SIDE BY SIDE

Italian
& English
GRAMMAR

SIDE BY SIDE

Italian & English

GRAMMAR

Paola Nanni-Tate and
C. Frederick Farrell Jr., PhD

New York   Chicago   San Francisco   Lisbon   London   Madrid   Mexico City
Milan   New Delhi   San Juan   Seoul   Singapore   Sydney   Toronto

1 2 3 4 5 6 7 8 9 10 11 12 13 14 15 16 17   QDB/QDB   1 9 8 7 6 5 4 3 2

ISBN   978-0-07-179733-7
MHID   0-07-179733-5

e-ISBN   978-0-07-179734-4
e-MHID   0-07-179734-3

Library of Congress Control Number 2012953140

Interior design by Village Bookworks

McGraw-Hill products are available at special quantity discounts to use as premiums
and sales promotions or for use in corporate training programs. To contact a
representative, please e-mail us at bulksales@mcgraw-hill.com.

This book is printed on acid-free paper.

Contents

Preface

Side by Side Italian & English Grammar presents the essential elements of Italian grammar—usually covered in a high school program or in the first year of college Italian—"side by side" with their English counterparts. This comparative/contrastive approach allows students to build on what they already know, as they see the ways in which English and Italian are similar, and to avoid potential trouble spots.

Side by Side Italian & English Grammar has been used in both high school and college Italian classes, and even in some English classes for a few students who were having trouble in understanding their English grammar text. Its vocabulary is, for the most part, limited to the 1,500 most frequently used Italian words.

This book has been used as

1. a reference book for beginning students, for whom the standard works are too complex to be useful. This allows students a means for independent inquiry.

2. a means of quick review of material forgotten over the summer or material missed because of illness.

3. a means of helping a student in a new school catch up with the class.

4. a means of organizing or summarizing material presented in the primary text, especially for students whose learning style favors an "organized approach."

5. a means of providing a common background for talking about language with students who have studied English in different ways, so that their study of Italian will show them something about how language works, one of the expectations of many college language requirements.

6. an alternative method of explaining grammatical points in both English and Italian to relieve the classroom teacher of the task.

Special features of the book that students will find useful include

1. a standard format that introduces each part of speech and answers the most common questions about it.

2. Quick Check charts that allow students to express themselves with more confidence, since they can independently check their sentences against a model.

3. appendices that identify and summarize trouble spots, such as the differences between the forms of the interrogative pronouns and adjectives.

4. an exercise section that tests understanding of the main grammatical areas covered in the book.

We hope that this text will provide ways for students to increase their independent work and to adapt material to their own learning styles and situations.

Introduction

The purpose of this book is to help you learn Italian more easily.

Many students have had trouble with foreign languages because they have not looked carefully enough, or critically enough, at their own. Struggles with your own language took place at such an early age that you have forgotten the times when it seemed difficult. Now it seems perfectly natural to you, and it is hard to adapt to different ways of expressing ideas.

The material in this book has been classified and arranged to show you English and your new language "side by side." You may be surprised at how many grammatical elements are similar in the two languages.

Information that is the same for both English and Italian is usually not repeated on facing pages. If you find that a section is omitted for the Italian, look to your left and find it on the English page. The English meaning of an Italian example is usually on the left-hand page, too.

Why grammar?

People can speak, read, or write their native language, at least to a reasonable degree, without studying formal grammar (the rules governing how we say, change, and arrange words to express our ideas). Just by being around other speakers, we hear millions of examples, and the patterns we hear become a part of us. Even babies start with correct basic patterns (subject-verb-object), even though words may be missing or incorrect: "Me wants cookie!"

Knowledge of grammar helps a great deal, though, in testing new and more complex words or patterns and in analyzing one's writing to discover where a sentence went wrong or how it could be more effective. Sometimes, "It sounds right (or wrong)" won't help.

All of the explanations in this book reflect standard English or Italian. You may sometimes think, "I don't say that!" The important word here is "say." We often ignore some rules in conversation, or even in informal writing such as friendly letters. When you are writing an important paper or giving a speech, however, you may want to use the standard form in order to make the best possible impression. You will also find that knowing grammar will help you in your study of language.

In learning a foreign language, grammar is necessary because it tells you how to choose the right word—or the right form of a word that you are using for the first time. It is not the way that you acquired your native language as a child, but it is an efficient way for adults who want to express more complex ideas and do not want to make any more mistakes than absolutely necessary.

Grammar saves you time and prevents many mistakes by guiding you in your choices.

SIDE BY SIDE

Italian & English

GRAMMAR

Introducing languages

A short history of English

What we now know as England was settled in the fifth and sixth centuries A.D. by Germanic tribes like the Angles, the Saxons, and the Jutes—all speaking related, but distinct, dialects. Later, in the ninth century, Scandinavian invaders came, bringing their languages, which also contributed to English. Political power determined the centers of learning, which contained the literature of continental Europe, written in Latin, as well as contributions of the inhabitants of Britain. By the ninth century, the primary center was in Wessex, due to the Viking invasions in the north, and so the West Saxon dialect became standard as Old English. It was heavily inflected, with endings on nouns to show many cases and on verbs to show time and person.

This was the language current in 1066, when William the Conqueror, from the province of Normandy in what is now France, won the battle of Hastings and became ruler of England. The natives knew no French; William and his followers did not speak Old English. For a long time, each group continued to speak its own language, but gradually they merged. Since the governing group spoke French, we often find that words for work, home, and ordinary things come from Old English, while words for leisure or artistic goods come from French.

Wamba, the jester in Sir Walter Scott's *Ivanhoe,* made a joke about this, saying that cows and pigs were Anglo-Saxon while the peasants took care of them, but became French (beef and pork) when they were ready to be eaten. In the same way, "house" looks and sounds like the German word *Haus,* but "mansion" looks like the French word for "house," *maison.*

English often uses several words with a similar meaning, with the more elegant word frequently being of French origin. For example, instead of "give," we may say "donate," which is like the French *donner*; instead of "mean," we may say "signify," from French *signifier.*

Latin, the language of the church and therefore of learning in general throughout all Europe, also had an influence on English. Around 1500, English absorbed about 25 percent of known Latin vocabulary. English, therefore, is basically a Germanic language, but one to which large portions of French and Latin were added.

Since the French also borrowed from Latin in the Renaissance, the languages have many words in common, but they are not the everyday words. Compare the following.

GERMANIC ROOT (COMMON)	FRENCH ROOT (ELEGANT)	LATIN ROOT (LEARNED)
ask	*question*	*interrogate*
goodness	*virtue*	*probity*
better	*improve*	*ameliorate*
rider	*cavalier*	*equestrian*

A short history of Italian

Italian is one of the Romance languages, like Spanish, French, and others that have developed from Latin and are the direct offspring of the Latin spoken by the Romans and by the people under their dominion. Of all the major Romance languages, Italian bears the closest resemblance to Latin.

As Italian evolved, many dialects sprang up. The multiplicity of these dialects presented a peculiar difficulty in the evolution of a form of Italian that would be widely accepted and that would reflect the cultural unity of the Italian peninsula. For several centuries, Italian writers published their work in their native dialects, producing a number of competing regional schools of literature.

Modern Italian developed from the Florentine dialect, which began to predominate in the fourteenth century because of the geographic centrality of Tuscany on the Italian peninsula, as well as the dominant commercial position of Florence. Slowly, the Florentine dialect began to be used by educated people, and by the second half of the sixteenth century, it was adopted as the common written language for the entire country. Florentine culture had produced the three literary artists who best represent Italian culture through the late Middle Ages to the early Renaissance: Dante, Petrarca, and Boccaccio.

By the nineteenth century, the language spoken by educated Tuscans spread and became the language of the new nation. The unification of Italy in 1861 had a large impact—not only politically, but also socially, economically, and culturally. With mandatory schooling, the literacy of the country increased, and many citizens abandoned their native dialect in favor of the national language.

All languages change, and the trend is to inflect them less and less. Distinctions that seem unnecessary or difficult may die out. Some languages retain such distinctions, and others—over time—abandon them. For example, in Latin and German, every noun had gender, number, and case, which indicated its function (that is, how it was used in the sentence). German still has all three as very important elements, while Italian and other Romance languages no longer show case in nouns.

In English, we pay little attention to grammatical gender, but nouns still have number (singular and plural) and one extra case (the possessive), while pronouns also have an objective case (*him/her*, as opposed to *he/she*). The functions of other cases are expressed by word order and prepositions. Italian no longer has cases for nouns, but it does have grammatical gender and number. Italian adjectives also have different endings, reflecting the gender and number of the nouns they modify.

Let's compare Latin, Italian, and English forms in the present tense conjugation of the verb "to have."

LATIN		MODERN ITALIAN		MODERN ENGLISH	
habeo	*habemus*	*io ho*	*noi abbiamo*	*I have*	*we have*
habes	*habetis*	*tu hai*	*voi avete*	*you have*	*you have*
habet	*habent*	*lui/lei ha*	*loro hanno*	*he/she has*	*they have*

You will notice that there are both differences and similarities in the conjugations. The Latin endings are so distinctive that it is not necessary to indicate the subject of the verb. This is also true of modern languages like Spanish and Italian. In English, the subject must always be expressed, whether it is a noun or a pronoun.

H is often not pronounced in many European languages, and never in Italian.

Modern English is the least inflected of the modern languages referenced here, French is next, then Italian, Spanish, and German.

The Italian alphabet consists of 21 letters, five of which are vowels, plus the letters *j, k, w, x,* and *y,* which are used only in Italian words of foreign origin.

2

Parts of speech

Introducing the parts of speech

Both English and Italian words are categorized by parts of speech. You may have learned these in elementary school without understanding their usefulness. They are important, because different rules apply to the different categories. In your own language, you do this naturally, unless the word is new to you. You know to say *one horse, two horses,* adding an *-s* to make the noun *horse* plural. You do not try to apply a noun's rule to a verb and say *I am, we ams;* instead, you say *we are.* People learning a foreign language sometimes use the wrong set of rules, however, because all of the forms are new, so nothing "sounds wrong." To avoid this kind of mistake, learn the part of speech when you learn a new vocabulary word.

Parts of speech help you identify words, so that even if a word is used in several ways (and this happens in both English and Italian), you can determine the Italian equivalent. For instance, *that* can be

1. a conjunction.

    *I know **that** Mary is coming.*
    *Io so **che** Maria viene.*

2. a demonstrative adjective.

    ***That** person is impossible.*
    ***Quella** persona è impossibile.*

3. a pronoun.

    *I didn't know **that**.*
    *Non sapevo **quello**.*

When you know the parts of speech, the fact that a word is used several ways in English won't cause you to choose the wrong one in Italian.

Following is a list of the parts of speech. The parts are described (1) in traditional definitions, (2) by the forms that identify them, and (3) by their functions (as structural linguists think of them).

Nouns

1. Names or words standing for persons, places, things, or abstract concepts

    John
    man
    Rome
    city
    table
    justice

2. Words that become plural by adding *-s* or *-es* (in addition to a few other ways)

    book ~ books
    fox ~ foxes
    child ~ children

3. Words that function as subjects, objects, or complements

    ***John** is here.*
    *She read the **book**.*
    *There is **Mary**.*

Pronouns

1. Words that substitute for nouns

    *John is already here. Have you seen **him**?*

2. Words that are used when no noun is identified

    ***It** is raining.*
    ***They** say . . .*
    ***You** never know.*

3. Words that serve the same function as nouns

    ***He** is here.*
    ***He** loves **her**.*
    *There **it** is.*

Adjectives

1. Words that modify, limit, or qualify a noun or pronoun

    dumb
    red
    serious
    happy

2. Words that may be inflected (may change form) or may be preceded by *more* or *most* to make comparisons

    dumb ~ dumber ~ dumbest
    *serious ~ **more** serious ~ **most** serious*

Adverbs

1. Words that modify verbs, adjectives, or other adverbs by telling how, when, where, or how much

    *We'll come **soon**.*
    *It's **really** big.*
    *They do it **very** well.*

2. Words that can show comparison between verbs (as adjectives do for nouns)

    soon ~ sooner ~ soonest
    *rapidly ~ **more** rapidly ~ **most** rapidly*

Conjunctions

1. Coordinating conjunctions (for example, *and, but,* and *so*) connect words, phrases, or clauses that are grammatically equivalent.

    *John **and** Mary*
    *on the table, **but** under a napkin*
    *I had no money, **so** I stayed at home.*

2. Subordinating conjunctions (for example, *if, because,* and *when*) connect subordinate clauses to the main clause of a sentence.

    ***When** you see it, you will believe me.*

Interjections

1. Exclamations

    Hey!
    Wow!

2. Words that can be used alone or in sentences

    Darn!
    ***Oh,** Mary, is it true?*

Prepositions

1. Words that express place, time, and other circumstances and show the relationship between two elements in a sentence

    at
    for
    in
    of
    on
    to

2. Words that are not inflected (never change form)

3. Words that have a noun or pronoun as their object

    ***in** a minute*
    ***of** a sort*
    ***on** it*

These groups are called prepositional phrases.

Verbs

1. Words that express action, existence, or state of being

    speak
    learn
    run
    be
    have
    feel

2. Words that may be inflected to show person (*I **am** ~ he **is***), time (*I **sing** ~ I **sang***), voice (*I **write** ~ it is **written***), and mood (*if I **am** here ~ if I **were** you*)

Nouns

English Introducing nouns

Definition   See page 6.

Forms   English nouns are considered to have gender, number, and case.

GENDER Masculine or feminine gender is used only for someone or something that is male or female.

man
woman
bull
tigress

All other nouns are neuter. Gender makes no difference in English except when there are two forms for one noun (for example, *actor* and *actress*) or when the nouns are replaced by pronouns (for example, *he, she, it*).

NUMBER Most nouns add *-s* or *-es* to the singular form to form the plural.

train ~ trains
box ~ boxes

Some nouns have irregular plural forms.

mouse ~ mice
man ~ men
child ~ children

CASE There is only one extra case in English: the possessive, or genitive. It is formed by adding *-'s* to a singular noun or *-'* to a plural noun ending in *-s*.

Mary's *book*
*the **book's** cover*
*the **books'** covers*

The possessive case can often be ignored, and *of* used instead, although this form is less common when a person is involved.

*Kant's theories → the theories **of Kant***
*the book's pages → the pages **of the book***

Nouns are often preceded by determiners (see page 16).

a *book,* ***the*** *book,* ***my*** *book,* ***two*** *books*

Uses   The three most common uses of nouns are as subjects, objects, and complements (see page 14).

SUBJECT	***Mrs. Pellegrini*** *is Italian.*
APPOSITIVE	*Mrs. Pellegrini, an Italian **woman**, is visiting us.*
DIRECT OBJECT OF A VERB	*He has a **pencil**.*
INDIRECT OBJECT OF A VERB	*She gave the hat to **Paul**.*
OBJECT OF A PREPOSITION	*We are in the **room**.*
COMPLEMENT	*It is a valuable **book**.*
ADJECTIVE	*I have my **history** textbook.*

CONTINUED ON PAGE 12 ▶

Italian · Introducing nouns

Definition See page 6.

Forms Italian nouns are considered to have gender and number, but not case.

> **GENDER** All nouns in Italian are either masculine or feminine; there are no neuter nouns. When you learn an Italian noun, you must also learn whether it is masculine or feminine.
>
> The gender of nouns is very important in Italian, since their determiners and the adjectives accompanying them must be of the same gender. If a noun is preceded by *il, lo, un,* or *uno,* it is masculine; *la* and *una* designate a feminine noun. *L'* and *un'* are used before a word beginning with a vowel or *h* to make it easier to say. *L'* and *un'* do not tell you which gender the word is.
>
> **NUMBER** An Italian noun that ends in *-o* or *-e* changes this ending to *-i* to form the plural. A noun ending in *-a* changes this ending to *-e* to form the plural. Plural nouns also require a plural article. *I* is the plural for *il, gli* is the plural for *lo,* and *le* is the plural for *la.*
>
> | | |
> |---|---|
> | *il maestro* | the teacher |
> | *i maestri* | the teachers |
> | *lo studente* | the student |
> | *gli studenti* | the students |
> | *la casa* | the home |
> | *le case* | the homes |
> | *una penna* | a pen |
>
> Several common nouns are exceptions to these rules.
>
> Family nouns do not change in the plural; instead, they are preceded by the plural article *i* (for example, *i Pellegrini*).
>
> **CASE** Italian nouns do not have different cases. Possession is indicated by the preposition *di,* plus an article if one is needed.
>
> > *le teorie **di Kant***
> > *le pagine **del libro***
>
> Italian nouns are often preceded by determiners (see page 17).
>
> > ***un** libro, **il** libro, **il mio** libri, **due** libri*

Uses Nouns are used in the same way in Italian and English. Compare the following sentences with the English sentences on the opposite page.

> ***La signora Pellegrini** è italiana.*
> *La signora Pellegrini, una **donna** italiana, viene a visitarci.*
> *Lui ha una **matita**.*
> *Lei ha dato il cappello a **Paolo**.*
> *Siamo nella **camera**.*
> *È un **libro** prezioso.*
> *Ho il mio testo **di storia**.*

Rarely is an Italian noun used alone as an adjective; a phrase, usually with *di, da,* or *in,* is used.

CONTINUED ON PAGE 13 ▶

Types   There are several ways to classify nouns. Following are two important ones.

1. Common vs. proper

   Common nouns are applied to a class of individuals. They begin with a lowercase letter.

   > *student*
   > *country*
   > *cat*
   > *language*

   Proper nouns name a specific individual within a class. They begin with a capital letter.

   > *Miss Jones*
   > *Italy*
   > *Kitty*
   > *English*

2. Countable vs. mass

   Countable nouns can be counted.

   > *one pencil*
   > *two sharks*
   > *three engineers*

   Mass nouns cannot be separated into individuals—they cannot be counted.

   > *salt*
   > *weather*
   > *sadness*

Italian Introducing nouns (continued)

Types   Italian nouns may be classified as follows.

1. Common vs. proper

   For the most part, Italian is the same as English in this classification, but there are a few important differences. Nouns for languages, days of the week, and months are common nouns in Italian and do not require a capital letter.

l'inglese	English
lunedì	Monday
ottobre	October

2. Countable vs. mass

   This classification follows the same principle in Italian as in English. However, mass nouns like *la gente* and *il pubblico* are treated as singular. In addition, nouns of this classification frequently require a partitive construction in Italian (see page 18).

Introducing subjects and objects

Subjects

Subjects are most frequently nouns or pronouns. The subject of a verb is the person or thing that *is* something or *is doing* something.

> *Mary* and *I* *are here.*
> *John* *speaks Italian.*
> *Are they* (the textbooks) *arriving today?*

 QUICK CHECK

Ask yourself: *Who* is here? *Who* speaks Italian? *What* is arriving?

Answer: the subject

In normal word order, the subject comes before the verb. The subject is usually, but not always, the first word in a sentence or clause.

Subject complements

Subject complements are words or phrases that define, or complete an idea about, the subject.

> *Mr. White is a **professor**.*
> *Jeanne and Alice are **Americans**.*

Direct objects

Some systems of grammar refer to direct objects as "object complements." The name matters less than the ability to recognize their important function. Direct objects are usually nouns or pronouns that directly receive the verb's action. In normal word order, the direct object comes after the verb.

> *Mary likes **John**. She likes **him**.*
> *The professor is giving a **test**. He is giving **it**.*

 QUICK CHECK

Ask yourself: *Who* is liked? *What* is being given?

Answer: the direct object

Indirect objects

Indirect objects are usually nouns or pronouns that are indirectly affected by the verb's action. They indicate *to* whom or *for* whom something is done.

> *Speak **to me**!*

Verbs of communication often have implied direct objects, as in *Tell me (the news)*. These objects are sometimes expressed in other languages.

COMBINATIONS Some verbs (for example, *give, tell,* and *buy*) can have more than one object. In addition to a direct object, there can be an indirect object. Counting the subject, there can be three nouns or pronouns with different functions, even in a short sentence.

> *Robert gives* **the book** *to Alice.*
> SUBJECT   DIRECT OBJECT   INDIRECT OBJECT
>
> *Robert gives* **Alice**   *the book.*
> SUBJECT   INDIRECT OBJECT   DIRECT OBJECT
>
> *He gives* **it**   *to her.*
> SUBJECT   DIRECT OBJECT   INDIRECT OBJECT

Notice that the two possible word orders have no effect on which object is direct and which is indirect. The word order in English simply determines whether or not the word *to* is used.

 QUICK CHECK

To analyze the sentences above, ask yourself: *Who gives?*

Answer: *Robert* or *he* (the subject)

Who or *what* is given?

Answer: *the book* or *it* (the direct object)

To/for whom / to/for what is it given?

Answer: *Alice* or *her* (the indirect object)

Objects of prepositions

All prepositions must have objects (see page 7). These objects come immediately after the preposition.

> on the **table** ~ on **it**
> after **Peter** ~ after **him**

In questions and relative clauses in English (see page 76), this rule is often ignored, and the preposition is used alone at the end of the sentence.

> **To whom** did you give it?
> → **Whom** did you give it **to**?

The first sentence is considered standard English. Italian uses the same patterns as standard English.

Problems with direct and indirect objects

English and Italian verbs with the same meaning usually take the same kind of object, but not always. The exceptions must be learned as vocabulary items. See the chart below for examples.

Comparison of objects in English and Italian

DIRECT OBJECT IN ENGLISH	INDIRECT OBJECT IN ITALIAN
He **obeys** his parents.	*Lui **ubbidisce ai** suoi genitori.*
He **phones** Ann.	*Lui **telefona a** Anna.*
I **am answering** the letter.	*Io **rispondo alla** lettera.*
Mary always **asks** John.	*Maria **chiede** sempre **a** Giovanni.*

OBJECT OF A PREPOSITION IN ENGLISH	DIRECT OBJECT IN ITALIAN
Irene **is looking at** the book.	*Irene **guarda** il libro.*
Monica **is looking for** the book.	*Monica **cerca** il libro.*
Michael **is waiting for** the train.	*Michele **aspetta** il treno.*
The student **listens to** the radio.	*Lo studente **ascolta** la radio.*

Definition   Determiners are words that introduce nouns and their adjectives. They usually come first in a noun phrase.

> **the** red book
> **a** tall boy
> **each** window
> **several** students

Types   Many kinds of words can serve as determiners: definite articles, indefinite articles, partitives, numbers, and general words like *each, either,* and *several.* Some types of adjectives (possessives, demonstratives, and interrogatives) can also be determiners; these are discussed in Chapter 5.

Forms   The **definite article** is always written *the,* but it is pronounced like *thee* before words beginning with a vowel or silent *h* (*the book* vs. *the apple, the hour*). The **indefinite article** is *a* or *an* in the singular, *some* in the plural. *An* is used before words beginning with a vowel or silent *h.* Other forms of determiners do not change their spelling or pronunciation.

Uses   DEFINITE ARTICLES   *The* indicates a specific noun.

> **The** book (the one you wanted) *is on the table.*

INDEFINITE ARTICLES   *A/an* refers to any individual in a class.

> I see **a** boy (not a specific one).

OTHER DETERMINERS   The use of other determiners is governed by their meaning.

> **some** boys
> **few** boys
> **several** boys
> **eight** boys

 Introducing determiners

Forms **DEFINITE ARTICLES** The form of the Italian definite article depends on the gender and number of its noun and on whether the noun begins with a consonant or vowel.

	BEFORE A CONSONANT	BEFORE A VOWEL	BEFORE **Z** OR **S** + CONSONANT
MASCULINE SINGULAR	*il* giorno	*l'*ufficio	*lo* studente
MASCULINE PLURAL	*i* giorni	*gli* uffici	*gli* studenti
FEMININE SINGULAR	*la* televisione	*l'*amica	
FEMININE PLURAL	*le* televisioni	*le* amiche	

These forms can also be combined with the prepositions *a, da, di, in,* and *su* (see page 75).

INDEFINITE ARTICLES The indefinite article agrees with its noun in gender, just as the definite article does. If the noun is feminine and begins with a vowel, the indefinite article is *un'*. Indefinite articles are used only with singular nouns.

	BEFORE A CONSONANT	BEFORE A VOWEL	BEFORE **Z** OR **S** + CONSONANT
MASCULINE SINGULAR	*un* giorno	*un* amico	*uno* studente
FEMININE SINGULAR	*una* televisione	*un'*amica	

PARTITIVES Partitives are normally formed by the preposition *di* plus the appropriate definite article.

del pane	(some) bread
dello zucchero	(some) sugar
della frutta	(some) fruit
*dell'*acqua	(some) water
dei bambini	(some) children
delle case	(some) houses

Note that after an expression including *di,* the article is not added.

Ho bisogno di soldi.	I need (some) money.
Ho bisogno di amici.	I need (some) friends.

OTHER DETERMINERS Every determiner must be learned as a separate vocabulary item. Some determiners change their spelling for gender or number; be sure to check as you learn new words.

ogni	each, every; all
tutto/tutta/tutti/tutte	every; all
ciascun/ciascuno/ciascuna	each, every

CONTINUED ON PAGE 18 ▶

Uses   **Definite articles** are used

1. before a specific noun, as in English.

2. before a noun used in a general sense.

> *Io detesto **la** televisione.*   I hate television (generally speaking).
> *I **film** di guerra sono spaventosi.*   War movies (in general) are frightening.

3. before many kinds of nouns that take no article in English.

LANGUAGES	*l'inglese*
QUALITIES	*la bellezza*
COUNTRIES	*l'Italia*
TITLES	*il generale*
MODIFIED PROPER NAMES	*la vecchia Roma, **la** piccola Isabella*

After certain verbs, such as *parlare* and *studiare,* the article is generally omitted.

> *Stefano parla **italiano**.*
> *Marcella studia **francese**.*

Indefinite articles are used

1. for the number "one."

> ***un** bambino*
> ***una** bambina*

2. for any member of a group or category.

> *Paolo ha **un** buon professore.*

Partitives are used to express part of a whole. English, which does not make this distinction, usually places no determiner before the noun.

> *I **soldi** sono utili.*   Money (in general) is useful.
> *Io ho **dei** soldi.*   I have (some) money.

Since English typically uses the single word *money* in these cases, we have to stop and think. Do we mean *all* money or money *in general* (and therefore use only the definite article in Italian), or do we mean just *some* money (what we have today, for example), in which case we use the partitive? Following are additional examples.

> *Mi piace **il** gelato. **Il** gelato è buono.*   I like ice cream. (All) ice cream is good.

Much as I like it, however, I can consume only a *part* of this whole quantity.

> *Vorrei **del** gelato, per piacere.*   I'd like some ice cream, please.

The definite article is used to refer to a group as a whole.

> ***Gli** studenti all'università sono*   (All) students at the university are
> *intelligenti.*   intelligent.

But it is not used to refer to a *part* of a group.

> *Ci sono **degli** studenti nella classe.*   There are students in the classroom.

OTHER DETERMINERS Most other Italian determiners are used as they are in English. Many, however, change form to agree with the noun in gender and number. Differences are noted in dictionaries and vocabulary lists. See Appendix D.

4

Pronouns

Definition   See page 6.

Forms   Like nouns, English pronouns have gender, number, and case, but further distinctions can be made. They also show person.

PERSON   English distinguishes three persons. **First person** is the one who is speaking (*I, me, we, us*). **Second person** is the one being spoken to (*you*). **Third person** is the one being spoken about (*he, him, she, her, it, they, them*). Both pronouns and verbs are listed according to person.

GENDER   Some, but not all, pronouns can be distinguished by gender. *I* can refer to either a man or a woman. *She*, however, is always feminine, *he* is always masculine, and *it*, even if it refers to an animal, is always neuter.

NUMBER   Each of the three persons may be either singular or plural.

CASE   Pronouns show more cases than nouns: the subjective (for example, *I* and *she*), the possessive (for example, *my/mine* and *her/hers*), and the objective (*me* and *her*). These are discussed below, under Uses.

Uses   Personal pronouns have the same functions as nouns.

1. Subject

   She *is here.*

2. Direct object

   *I like **them**.*

3. Indirect object

   *I am giving **him** the book.*

4. Object of a preposition

   *The question is hard for **me**.*

5. Complement

   *It is **she** who is speaking.*

Types   There are several types of pronouns.

1. Personal (page 22)

2. Possessive (page 26)

3. Reflexive/reciprocal (page 28)

4. Disjunctive (page 30)

5. Relative (page 32)

6. Demonstrative (page 36)

7. Interrogative (page 38)

Italian Introducing pronouns

Definitions, forms, and uses are the same for Italian and English pronouns. However, there are two important differences to be aware of.

1. In Italian, the personal pronoun for "you" has two forms in the singular—the familiar (*tu*) and the formal (*Lei*). The plural forms are *voi* and *Loro*, respectively.

    Tu is the familiar form of "you" and is generally used to address the following.

    > A member of your family
    > A close friend
    > A fellow student or colleague
    > A small child
    > An inferior (sometimes as an insult)
    > An animal
    > God

    Lei is universally recognized as the polite or formal way to say "you." It is used to address anyone who does not fall into one of the categories listed above. It is used to address both males and females, whether meeting people for the first time, addressing older people, or in business situations. In writing, *Lei* is capitalized. If you are uncertain about which form of "you" to use, use *Lei* first, then follow the lead of the native speaker, or wait until the person asks you to use the informal pronoun *tu*.

    Voi is the plural form corresponding to *tu* and is used to address a group of people with whom you have a friendly relationship.

    Loro is the plural form of *Lei*. It is used to address both males and females, as well as a group that includes both males and females. It is also used to address a group of people you do not know well. In writing, *Loro* is capitalized.

    In contemporary Italian, *voi* is used as the plural of both *tu* and *Lei*; *Loro* is generally reserved for very formal situations.

2. There is no neuter gender in Italian; *il, lo* replaces masculine things as well as people, and *la* replaces feminine ones. In the plural, *i* and *gli* are used both for groups of masculine people or things and for mixed groups; *le* is used only for all-feminine groups.

English Personal pronouns

Subject pronouns (see page 14)

	SINGULAR	PLURAL
FIRST PERSON	*I*	*we*
SECOND PERSON	*you*	*you*
THIRD PERSON	*he, she, it, one* (indefinite)	*they*

John gives a present. → *He gives it.* (third-person singular)
Mary and I arrive. → *We arrive.* (first-person plural)

Direct object pronouns (see page 14)

	SINGULAR	PLURAL
FIRST PERSON	*me*	*us*
SECOND PERSON	*you*	*you*
THIRD PERSON	*him, her, it, one*	*them*

*He sees **me**, and I see **you**.*
*You will find **them**.*

CONTINUED ON PAGE 24 ▶

 ## Personal pronouns

Subject pronouns (see page 14)

In Italian, a subject pronoun must always be of the same gender and number as the noun that it replaces.

	SINGULAR	PLURAL
FIRST PERSON	*io*	*noi*
SECOND PERSON	*tu*	*voi*
THIRD PERSON	*lui* (m.), *lei* (f.), *Lei*	*loro, Loro*

Note the lowercase *i* of *io* in the first-person singular.

Direct object pronouns (see page 14)

	SINGULAR	PLURAL
FIRST PERSON	*mi*	*ci*
SECOND PERSON	*ti*	*vi*
THIRD PERSON	*lo* (m.), *la* (f.), *La*	*li* (m.), *le* (f.), *Li, Le*

*Lui **mi** vede, e io **ti** vedo.*
*Tu **le** troverai.*

The final vowel of a singular form may elide (be dropped) before a vowel or *h*.

| *Lui **m'**ama.* | He loves me. |
| *Lui **l'**ha vista.* | He saw her. |

Note that it is possible, but not necessary, to elide singular direct object pronouns in such cases.

| ***Mi** ama, non **mi** ama.* | He loves me, he loves me not. |
| OR ***M'**ama, non **m'**ama.* | |

POSITION Except in infinitive constructions and affirmative commands, an object pronoun in Italian is placed directly before the conjugated verb of which it is the object.

*Lui **mi** vede. Io **ti** vedo.*	He sees me. I see you.
Cerco il libro.	I am looking for the book.
→ ***Lo** cerco.*	I am looking for it.
Maria compra i libri.	Mary buys the books.
→ *Maria **li** compra.*	Mary buys them.

The object pronoun is also placed directly before the verb in a question or in a negative sentence.

Hai i biglietti?	Do you have the tickets?
→ ***Li** hai?*	Do you have them?
Non ho i biglietti.	I don't have the tickets.
→ *Non **li** ho.*	I don't have them.

CONTINUED ON PAGE 25 ▶

Indirect object pronouns (see page 14)

	SINGULAR	PLURAL
FIRST PERSON	*(to/for) me*	*(to/for) us*
SECOND PERSON	*(to/for) you*	*(to/for) you*
THIRD PERSON	*(to/for) him, her, it, one*	*(to/for) them*

*They send the letter **to us**.*
*He writes **her** a letter.*
*I bought a dress **for her**.*
*I got **them** a ticket.*

Objects of prepositions (see page 15)

After a preposition, English uses the same form of the pronoun as for direct objects.

Be careful with compound pronoun subjects or objects. These remain in the same case as that for a single subject or object.

***I** am Italian. **She** and **I** are Italian.*
*This is between **us**. This is between **you** and **me**.*
*Give it to **them**. Give it to **him** and **her**.*

WORD ORDER When there are two pronoun objects in English, the direct object comes before the indirect object.

*He shows **it** to **them**.*

When a noun and a pronoun are used together, word order can vary.

He shows **the book** **to them**.
          DIRECT OBJECT   INDIRECT OBJECT

He shows **them** **the book**.
          INDIRECT OBJECT DIRECT OBJECT

Personal pronouns (continued)

The only exceptions are infinitive constructions and affirmative commands. The pronoun follows these verb forms and is attached to them. In negative commands, the pronoun remains before the verb or is attached to it.

Pietro vuole leggere il libro.	Peter wants to read the book.
→ *Pietro **lo** vuole leggere.*	Peter wants to read it.
OR *Pietro vuole legger**lo**.*	
Dai il libro a Maria.	Give the book to Mary.
→ *Dal**lo** a Maria.*	Give it to Mary.
*Non **lo** dare a Maria.* OR *Non dar**lo** a Maria.*	Don't give it to Mary.

For more information about pronouns with commands, see page 115.

Indirect object pronouns (see page 14)

The Italian indirect object is often used where English would use a preposition plus object.

	SINGULAR	PLURAL
FIRST PERSON	*mi*	*ci*
SECOND PERSON	*ti*	*vi*
THIRD PERSON	*gli* (m.), *le* (f.), *Le*	*gli* (m., f.), *Loro*

Indirect object pronouns are placed before the verb, just as direct object pronouns are.

***Le** ho comprato una giacca.*	I bought her a jacket.
	OR I bought a jacket for her.
*Lei **gli** scrive una lettera.*	She writes him a letter.
*Non **mi** mandano una lettera.*	They do not send me a letter.

Objects of prepositions (see page 15)

Most prepositions require the disjunctive pronouns in Italian (see page 31). However, there is a pronoun that replaces both a preposition and its object.

Ne replaces *di* plus a noun or pronoun.

*Lui ha bisogno **di soldi**.*	He needs some money.
→ *Lui **ne** ha bisogno.*	He needs some.
***Ne** ha?*	Do you have some?

WORD ORDER Some Italian verbs often have more than one pronoun object.

*Lui **ce lo** mostra.*	He shows it to us.
*Lei **me la** dà.*	She gives it to me.

Note that *mi, ti, ci,* and *vi* (and the reflexive pronoun *si*) become *me, te, ce,* and *ve* (and *se*), respectively, when they precede a direct object pronoun.

When there are two pronouns before the verb, the word order is as follows.

Pietro ci compra il libro.				Peter buys us the book.
Pietro	***ce***	***lo***	*compra.*	Peter buys it for us.
SUBJECT	INDIRECT OBJECT	DIRECT OBJECT	VERB	

When used before *lo, la, li,* or *le,* the indirect object pronouns *gli, le, and Le* become *glie* and the combination is written as one word.

*Pietro **glielo** compra.*	Peter buys it for him.

CONTINUED ON PAGE 27 ▶

 Possessive pronouns

Definition A possessive pronoun replaces a possessive adjective (or a noun in the possessive) plus a noun.

> It's **my book**. → It's **mine**.
> It's **Anne's car**. → It's **hers**.

Forms Possessive pronouns have person and number; in the third-person singular, they also have gender. They do not have case, that is, they have the same form no matter what function they perform in a sentence.

	SINGULAR	PLURAL
FIRST PERSON	*mine*	*ours*
SECOND PERSON	*yours*	*yours*
THIRD PERSON	*his, hers, its, one's*	*theirs*

If you know the person, gender, and number of the possessor (*Mary* in the example below), there is only one choice for the pronoun (in this example, *hers*).

> *You have your book; where is **Mary's** book (**her** book)?*

To avoid repeating *book*, it is replaced along with the possessive noun or adjective in front of it. Since *Mary's* (or *her*) is third-person singular feminine, *hers* is the correct pronoun.

> *You have your book; where is **hers**?*

When the verb is reflexive, the word order is as follows.

Pietro si mette la maglia.				Peter puts on the sweater.
Pietro **se**	**la**	*mette.*		He puts it on.
SUBJECT REFLEXIVE OBJECT	DIRECT OBJECT	VERB		

In an affirmative command, objects *follow* the verb and are attached to it. The indirect object comes before the direct object, regardless of person.

Portamelo!	Bring it to me!
Diglielo!	Tell it to him!

 QUICK CHECK

NORMAL WORD ORDER FOR DOUBLE OBJECT PRONOUNS

SUBJECT + *me* + *lo (l')* + VERB
         te   *la (l')*
         gli   *li*
         ce   *le*
         ve
         gli

 **Possessive pronouns**

Forms   In Italian, possessive pronouns have person and number as in English, but they also have gender changes for the singular and plural forms. "Person" means the possessor, while gender and number are determined by what is owned.

il libro di Maria	Mary's book	*le camicie di Giovanni*	John's shirts
il suo libro	her book	*le sue camicie*	his shirts
il suo	hers	*le sue*	his

Even though *Maria* is female, the possessive pronoun is masculine singular (*il suo libro, il suo*), because *libro* is masculine. Likewise, although *Giovanni* is male, *camicie* is feminine plural and therefore requires a feminine plural pronoun (*le sue camicie, le sue*).

	SINGULAR	PLURAL
FIRST PERSON	*il mio, la mia, i miei, le mie*	*il nostro, la nostra, i nostri, le nostre*
SECOND PERSON	*il tuo, la tua, i tuoi, le tue*	*il vostro, la vostra, i vostri, le vostre*
THIRD PERSON	*il suo, la sua, i suoi, le sue*	*il loro, la loro, i loro, le loro*

1. The possessive pronouns have the same forms as the possessive adjectives (see page 53).

   In Italian, the phrases are expressed as follows.

una mia amica	a friend of mine
un tuo libro	a book of yours

2. With the exception of *loro*, the possessive pronouns are not preceded by the definite article if the verb *essere* is used.

*Sono **vostri** questi libri?*	Are these your books?
*No, sono **suoi**.*	No, they are his.
*È **tua** questa rivista?*	Is this your magazine?
*Sì, è **mia**.*	Yes, it is mine.

Definition Reflexive pronouns are pronoun objects or complements that refer to the same person(s) or thing(s) as another element in the sentence, usually the subject.

Forms

	SINGULAR	PLURAL	RECIPROCAL
FIRST PERSON	*myself*	*ourselves*	*each other/one another*
SECOND PERSON	*yourself*	*yourselves*	*each other/one another*
THIRD PERSON	*himself, herself, itself, oneself*	*themselves*	*each other/one another*

Uses Reflexive pronouns are used as objects of verbs and prepositions.

Types A reflexive pronoun is normally used only when the subject acts directly on himself/herself or does something for himself/herself directly.

> ***Paul*** *cut* **himself**.
> ***I*** *told* **myself** *it didn't matter.*

Occasionally, reflexive pronouns are used idiomatically.

> ***They*** *always enjoy* **themselves**.

For mutual or reciprocal action, *each other* or *one another* is used. This expression does not change form.

> ***They*** *congratulated* **each other**.
> ***You*** *two saw* **each other** *last night.*

Reflexive/reciprocal pronouns can function as direct or indirect object pronouns.

> ***They*** *saw* **each other**.
> ***We*** *talked to* **each other** *yesterday.*

In English, reflexive and reciprocal objects are often omitted.

> *We* **talked** *yesterday. (To each other is understood.)*

Sometimes, a construction is used that requires no object.

> *Paul* **got hurt**. *(Hurt himself is understood.)*

However, consider the following sentence.

> *We washed this morning.*

If you have not heard the rest of the conversation, the meaning is ambiguous. The sentence may have either of the following meanings.

> *We washed ourselves (got washed).*
> *We washed our clothes (did the laundry).*

 # Reflexive/reciprocal pronouns

Forms   The forms of Italian reflexive/reciprocal pronouns are the same as the forms of the direct and indirect object pronouns, except for the third person.

	SINGULAR	PLURAL
FIRST PERSON	*mi, m'*	*ci*
SECOND PERSON	*ti, t'*	*vi*
THIRD PERSON	*si*	*si*

Reflexive/reciprocal pronouns are placed in the same position in a sentence as object pronouns.

Uses   These pronouns are used as objects (either direct or indirect) of the verb (see page 14). They can be either reflexive or reciprocal, meaning either "self" or "each other."

Si *parlano.*	They are talking to themselves.
	OR They are talking to each other.

If the meaning is not clear, *stesso/stessa/stessi/stesse* can be added to the reflexive pronoun to indicate a reflexive function. *L'uno all'altro / l'una all'altra* can be used to indicate a reciprocal function.

Reflexive/reciprocal pronouns can function as both direct and indirect object pronouns.

Mi *lavo il viso.* (*mi* = indirect object)	I wash my face.
Mi *lavo.* (*mi* = direct object)	I wash myself.

Many more reflexive verbs are used in Italian than in English, because transitive verbs must have objects in Italian.

Laviamo la macchina.	We wash the car.
Ci *laviamo.*	We wash ourselves.

Many Italian reflexive verbs are not translated with English reflexive pronouns.

Noi **ci** *fermiamo.*	We stop.

Some Italian verbs can be used either reflexively or nonreflexively.

Mi *vesto.*	I get dressed.
Vesto mio figlio.	I dress my son.

Definition   A disjunctive pronoun is not attached to a verb. (*Disjunctive* means "not joined.") It is used alone or as an extra word to give special emphasis or to intensify an impression.

Forms and uses   The form of a disjunctive pronoun depends on its use.

1. Used alone, the disjunctive pronoun is in the subjective case (if required) in formal English, and in the objective case for informal use.

   > *Who's there?* **I.** (formal; *I am* is understood)
   > **Me.** (informal)

2. As an intensifier, the reflexive pronoun is normally used.

   > *I'll do it* **myself!**
   > *He told me so* **himself.**

3. Sometimes, we merely raise our voices for emphasis.

   > **You** *do it!*

Italian Disjunctive pronouns

Forms When used alone, disjunctive pronouns have the same forms as the subject pronouns, but as objects of prepositions, they have the following forms.

	SINGULAR	PLURAL
FIRST PERSON	*me*	*noi*
SECOND PERSON	*te*	*voi*
THIRD PERSON	*lui, lei, Lei, sé* (reflexive)	*loro, Loro*

Uses Disjunctive pronouns may be used

1. alone.

    *Chi è? **Io**!*   Who is it? Me!

2. as a complement after *sei*.

    *Sei **tu**!*   It is you!

3. with *stesso* for emphasis.

    *Me l'ha detto **lui stesso**.*   He told me so himself.

4. after prepositions and conjunctions.

    *Ognuno **per sé**.*   Every man for himself.
    *Paolo è più grande **di te**.*   Paul is bigger than you.

5. with the preposition *da* ("by") + personal pronoun (= "on one's own," "(by) oneself").

    Vuoi una mano?   Can I help you?
    *No, grazie. Faccio **da me**.*   No, thanks. I'll do it (by) myself.

    In this expression, *sé* is interchangeable with *solo/sola/soli/sole* ("alone").

    Luisa è una bambina che vuole fare   Luisa is a girl who wants to do
        *tutto **da sé** / **da sola**.*   everything herself/alone.

English Relative pronouns

Definition   Relative pronouns begin a relative clause. They refer to a noun, called the antecedent, and usually come directly after that noun.

Forms   Relative pronouns have the following forms in English.

	SUBJECT	OBJECT	POSSESSIVE	INDIRECT OBJECT/PREPOSITIONAL OBJECT
PERSON	*who/that*	*whom/that*	*whose*	*to/by whom*
THING	*which/that*	*which/that*	*whose/*	*to/by which*
			of which	*where* (for place prepositions)
				when (for time prepositions)

The correct pronoun is determined by the following factors.

1. Whether the antecedent is a person or a thing

2. The function of the pronoun in the clause

3. For subjects and objects, whether the clause is restrictive or nonrestrictive

   A **restrictive clause** defines the noun. *That* is used, and the clause is not set off by commas.

   *The book **that** you just read is world-renowned.*

   Without the clause, you would not know which book is meant. It is an essential definition.

   A **nonrestrictive clause** describes the noun, rather than defines it. It is not necessary to form a complete sentence. *Who, whom,* or *which* is used, and the clause is set off by commas.

   *I promessi sposi, **which** the class is going to read, is famous.*

   The relative clause could be eliminated, and the sentence would still make sense. It is a nonessential description.

Uses   Relative pronouns have several uses.

1. They introduce clauses that give additional information about the antecedent.

2. They allow you to join two short sentences to make your writing smoother and to avoid repetition.

   Mrs. Pellegrini came yesterday. Mrs. Pellegrini is an expert pianist.
   → *Mrs. Pellegrini, **who** is an expert pianist, came yesterday.*

3. They can be subjects, direct objects, indirect objects, possessives, or objects of a preposition in the relative clause.

4. They are inflected only for case, not for person or number. Their form depends on their function in the clause.

   The function of the antecedent in the main clause has no effect on the form of the relative pronoun.

Italian Relative pronouns

Forms Relative pronouns have the following forms in Italian.

SUBJECT	OBJECT	PREPOSITIONAL OBJECT
che	*che*	*cui*

Il quale may be used instead of *che*. It is used to distinguish gender and number in sentences where there are two nouns to which the relative pronoun could refer. *Il quale* must agree in gender and number with its antecedent.

Unlike English, Italian does not use different pronouns to distinguish between restrictive and nonrestrictive clauses.

*Il libro **che avete letto** è famoso.*	The book that you have read is famous.
I promessi sposi, ***che la classe leggerà**, è una novella famosa.*	*I promessi sposi*, which the class is going to read, is a famous novel.

Relative pronouns are often omitted in English.

That's the man I saw yesterday.

In the sentence above, the relative pronoun "whom" is omitted.

Italian does not allow this.

*È l'uomo **che** ho visto ieri.*

All relative pronouns must have antecedents. If there isn't one, *il* is supplied.

*Non è venuto, **il che** mi ha sorpreso.*	He didn't come, which surprised me.

A relative pronoun can take any form of the verb in its clause. This is also true of English, but many people do not follow this practice.

*Sono io **che sono** ansioso.*	It is I who am anxious.
*Siamo noi **che veniamo**.*	We are the ones who are coming.

This can cause problems, because relative pronouns (in English and Italian) often look the same as interrogative pronouns (for example, "who?" and "what?"), which always take a verb in the third person.

*Chi **è** ansioso? Io.*	Who is worried? I am.
*Chi **arriva**? Noi.*	Who is coming? We are.

English How to analyze relative pronouns

Mr. Smith *is an excellent cook.* **Mr. Smith** *made **these pies.***
SUBJECT   COMPLEMENT   SUBJECT   DIRECT OBJECT

1. Find the repeated element. → *Mr. Smith*
2. Identify the function of the repeated element in the second sentence, which will become the relative clause. → the subject
3. Choose the relative pronoun. → *who* (person, subject)
4. Copy the first sentence through the antecedent. → *Mr. Smith . . .*
5. Put in the correct relative pronoun, in this case, *who.* → *Mr. Smith, who . . .*
6. Copy the rest of the second sentence (now a relative clause). → *Mr. Smith, who made these pies . . .*
7. Copy the rest of the first sentence. → *Mr. Smith, who made these pies, is an excellent cook.*

Other examples follow.

The ten books are on the table. I am reading them.
*The ten books **that** I am reading are on the table.*

> *That* is used because it
>
> 1. is the object of *am reading* in the clause (no commas).
> 2. refers to a thing.
> 3. is restrictive (defines which ten books).

Mr. Jones died today. I saw him yesterday.
*Mr. Jones, **whom** I saw yesterday, died today.*

> *Whom* is used because it
>
> 1. is the object of *I saw* (with commas).
> 2. refers to a person.
> 3. is nonrestrictive. (You already know who Mr. Jones is. This merely gives an extra fact about him.)

The student is asleep. I am speaking to that student.
*The student **to whom** I am speaking is asleep.*

> *To whom* is used because it
>
> 1. is the indirect object (no commas).
> 2. refers to a person.
> 3. is restrictive (defines which student).

The old house is falling down. I lived in that house as a child.
*The old house **where** (in which) I lived as a child is falling down.*

> *Where* is used because it
>
> 1. replaces a place preposition plus noun object (no commas).
> 2. refers to a thing. (*In which* is also correct.)

The woman lives in New York. I took her coat.
*The woman **whose** coat I took lives in New York.*

> *Whose* is used because it
>
> 1. is possessive (no commas).
> 2. refers to a person.
> 3. is restrictive (defines which woman).

Italian How to analyze relative pronouns

The important considerations are function in the clause and word order.

M. Lucchini è **un cuoco eccellente**.
SUBJECT   COMPLEMENT

M. Lucchini ha fatto **questa torta**.
SUBJECT   DIRECT OBJECT

1. Find the repeated element. → *M. Lucchini*

2. Identify the function of the repeated element in the second sentence, which will become the relative clause. → the subject

3. Choose the relative pronoun. → *che*

4. Copy the first sentence through the antecedent. → *M. Lucchini…*

5. Put in the relative pronoun (with preposition, if any) to replace the second *M. Lucchini*. → *M. Lucchini, che…*

6. Copy the rest of the second sentence (now a relative clause). → *M. Lucchini, che ha fatto questa torta,…*

7. Copy the rest of the first sentence. → *M. Lucchini, che ha fatto questa torta, è un cuoco eccellente.*

Try this with other sentences. Follow the same steps until they feel natural.

I libri sono sulla tavola. Li ho già letti.
I libri che ho già letto sono sulla tavola.

Il signor Pellegrini è morto oggi. L'ho visto ieri.
Il signor Pellegrini, che ho visto ieri, è morto oggi.

Lo studente si è addormentato. Io parlo a questo studente.
Lo studente a cui parlo si è addormentato.

La vecchia casa è stata demolita. Io vivevo in questa casa quando ero giovane.
La vecchia casa nella quale vivevo quando ero giovane, è stata demolita.

La donna vive a New York. Io ho preso la giacca di questa donna.
La donna, la cui giacca ho preso, vive a New York.

This may seem complicated, requiring a lot of thought. That is because people usually use many short sentences when speaking. Relative clauses are used mainly to vary written style—when you have time to think, cross something out, and write it in a different way.

 ## Demonstrative pronouns

Definition   Demonstrative pronouns point out someone or something.

Forms   There are four forms of the demonstrative pronoun in English.

SINGULAR	PLURAL
this (one)	*these*
that (one)	*those*

Uses   These pronouns distinguish only between what is near (*this, these*) and far (*that, those*) and between singular and plural. No changes are made for gender or case.

> *I can't decide which of the chairs to buy.*
> **This one** *is lovely, but* **that one** *is comfortable.*
> **This** *is lovely, but* **that** *is comfortable.*

 Demonstrative pronouns

Forms There are two demonstrative pronouns in Italian: *questo* ("this") and *quello* ("that"). Each of these pronouns has special forms for gender and number.

	SINGULAR	PLURAL
MASCULINE	*questo*	*questi*
	quello	*quelli*
FEMININE	*questa*	*queste*
	quella	*quelle*

Uses Demonstrative pronouns replace a demonstrative adjective plus its noun.

> **quel** *signore* → **quello**
> **questa** *signora* → **questa**
> **quei** *signori* → **quelli**
> **queste** *signore* → **queste**

For emphasis, *questo* and *quello* may be followed by *qui* or *lì*, respectively.

> *Quale vuoi?* **Questo qui** *o* **quello lì?**   Which one do you want? This one
>   or that one?

The pronoun *quello/quella/quelli/quelle* may be followed by the preposition *di* to express possession.

> *I figli di Maria stanno studiando,*   Mary's kids are studying, Silvia's are
> **quelli di** *Silvia guardano la televisione.*   watching television.

The pronoun *quello/quella/quelli/quelle* may also be followed by a relative clause.

> *Lui è* **quello che** *amo.*   He is the one (that) I love.

 QUICK CHECK

DEMONSTRATIVE ADJECTIVE + NOUN → DEMONSTRATIVE PRONOUN		
	SINGULAR	PLURAL
MASCULINE	*questo libro* → *questo*	*questi libri* → *questi*
	quel libro, quello studente → *quello*	*quei libri, quegli studenti* → *quelli*
FEMININE	*questa casa* → *questa*	*queste case* → *queste*
	quella casa → *quella*	*quelle case* → *quelle*

Notice that the masculine singular demonstrative pronoun is *quello* and the masculine plural is *quelli*, regardless of the initial consonant(s) of the noun being replaced.

English Interrogative pronouns

Definition   Interrogative pronouns ask a question.

Forms   Interrogative pronouns have different forms for people and things. The pronoun referring to people, *who*, is also inflected for case.

	PEOPLE	THINGS
SUBJECT	*who?*	*which?*
		what?
OBJECT	*whom?*	*which?*
		what?

No change is made for number. *Who?/whom?* and *what?* can refer to one or more than one.

Uses   The interrogative pronouns in English are used in the following ways.

1. Person as subject

   Who *is coming? John.* OR *The Smiths.*

2. Thing as subject

   What *is going on? A riot.*

3. Person as direct object

   Whom *did you see? John.*

4. Thing as direct object

   What *are you doing? My homework.*

5. Person as indirect object*

   To whom *are you speaking? To Mary.*

6. Person as object of a preposition

   With whom *are you going? With John.*

7. Thing as object of a preposition

   What *are you thinking **about**? About the music.*

As an interrogative pronoun, *which?* relates to choice. It can simply be *which?*, used in the singular or plural, or *which one(s)?*

> *Here are two books.* ***Which (one)*** *do you want?*
> *There are many good shops in town.* ***Which (ones)*** *do you like best?*

---

*To or for signals the indirect object. (To review the indirect object, see page 14.)

 Interrogative pronouns

Forms Interrogative pronouns are confusing in both English and Italian because the same word can be used for different purposes.

	SUBJECT	DIRECT OBJECT	OBJECT OF A PREPOSITION
PERSON	*chi?*	*chi?*	*chi?*
	Chi *è?*	**Chi** *guardate?*	**A chi** *parlate?*
THING	*che?*	*che?*	*che?*
	Che *succede?*	**Che** *fate?*	**Di che** *avete bisogno?*

In formal English, many speakers distinguish between *who?* (subject) and *whom?* (object). Italian does not make this distinction.

In Italian, *chi?* and *che?* can be both subjects and objects of a verb, as well as objects of a preposition.

Unlike in English, an Italian question never ends with a preposition.

Most question words are invariable. However, *quale?* ("which?") and *quanto/quanti* ("how much? / how many?") agree in gender and number with the nouns they replace. The different forms do not change for the three grammatical functions listed above. For the distinction between *che?* and *quale?*, see Appendix A.

Che?, cosa?, and *che cosa?* are interchangeable for "what?"

Uses The interrogative pronouns in Italian are used in the following ways.

1. Person as subject

    Chi *arriva?* **Chi** *è che arriva? Maria, Giovanni e Paolo.*

2. Thing as subject

    Che *succede? Niente.*

3. Person as direct object

    Chi *avete visto? Maria e Giovanni.*

4. Thing as direct object

    Che cosa *fate? Leggo la rivista.*

5. Person as indirect object

    A chi *parlavi? A Maria.*

6. Person as object of a preposition

    Con chi *andate al cinema? Con gli amici.*

7. Thing as object of a preposition

    A che cosa *pensi? Al mio lavoro.*

CONTINUED ON PAGE 40 ▶

Choice interrogatives

Another kind of interrogative pronoun relates to choice: *Which one(s)?* These forms agree in number with the noun they replace.

SINGULAR	PLURAL
quale	*quali*

These interrogatives offer a choice between possibilities.

*Ho tre riviste. **Quale** preferisci?*	I have three magazines. Which one do you want?
Ci sono molti negozi nella piazza. ***Quali** preferite?*	There are many shops in the square. Which ones do you prefer?

Adjectives

English Introducing adjectives

Definition   See page 7.

Forms   Some English adjectives are invariable, while others change form. These changes depend on adjective type. The types are discussed separately below.

Uses   Adjectives are primarily used as

1. modifiers of nouns or pronouns.

2. complements of either the subject or an object.

An adjective's function determines its position in a sentence.

1. As a modifier, an adjective usually comes before the noun or pronoun that it modifies.

   *Buy **that small white house**.*
         ADJECTIVES   NOUN

   *Buy the **blue**   one.*
          ADJECTIVE PRONOUN

2. As a modifier of an indefinite pronoun, an adjective follows the pronoun.

   Something   ***terrible*** *is happening.*
   INDEFINITE PRONOUN   ADJECTIVE

3. As a subject complement, an adjective follows the verb *to be* or the linking verb and describes the subject.

   *Mrs. Pellegrini **is**   **happy**.*
                FORM OF *to be* ADJECTIVE

   *They **seem**   **pleased**.*
        LINKING VERB   ADJECTIVE

4. As an object complement, an adjective follows the direct object noun or pronoun.

   *That made **the exam hard**.*
              NOUN   ADJECTIVE

   *We considered **him**   **crazy**.*
              PRONOUN ADJECTIVE

Types   Each of the following adjective types is discussed separately below.

1. Descriptive (page 44)

2. Proper (a kind of descriptive adjective) (page 50)

3. Limiting (includes demonstratives, possessives, interrogatives, indefinites, numbers, and determiners) (page 50)

Forms   An adjective in Italian agrees in gender and number with the noun it modifies. If an adjective describes a mixed group of nouns (masculine and feminine), the adjective is masculine plural.

Uses   As in English, Italian adjectives are used as modifiers and complements, but their position in a sentence is different (see page 47).

 **Descriptive adjectives**

Definition Descriptive adjectives describe a noun or pronoun.

Forms Many of these adjectives may be inflected to show comparison.

 Descriptive adjectives

Forms Many descriptive adjectives in Italian end in *-o* in the masculine singular and *-a* in the feminine singular. The plural is created by changing the *-o* to *-i* and the *-a* to *-e*. The masculine singular form is the one listed first in vocabulary lists and dictionaries.

	SINGULAR	PLURAL
MASCULINE	*buono*	*buoni*
FEMININE	*buona*	*buone*

However, there are several groups of adjectives that use other endings or have irregular forms.

1. Most descriptive adjectives that do not end in *-o/-a* in the singular have the same form for both the masculine and feminine forms—one ending in *-e*. The plural is formed by changing the *-e* of the singular form to *-i*. Examples follow.

SINGULAR	PLURAL	ENGLISH EQUIVALENT
facile	*facili*	easy
feroce	*feroci*	ferocious
grande	*grandi*	big, large
intelligente	*intelligenti*	intelligent

2. Adjectives that end in *-ista* have the same form for the masculine and feminine singular, but two forms for the plural.

MASCULINE SINGULAR	*Il signore è **ottimista**.*	The man is an optimist.
MASCULINE PLURAL	*I signori sono **ottimisti**.*	Men are optimistic.
FEMININE SINGULAR	*La signora è **ottimista**.*	The woman is an optimist.
FEMININE PLURAL	*Le signore sono **ottimiste**.*	Women are optimistic.

3. Adjectives that end in *-one* have four different forms.

MASCULINE SINGULAR	*un ragazzo **chiacchierone***	a talkative boy
MASCULINE PLURAL	*i ragazzi **chiacchieroni***	talkative boys
FEMININE SINGULAR	*una ragazza **chiacchierona***	a talkative girl
FEMININE PLURAL	*le ragazze **chiacchierone***	talkative girls

4. Adjectives that end in *-o* and indicate a geographical division are treated the same way as regular adjectives ending in *-o*. They have four forms (*-o/-a/-i/-e*). If a geographical adjective ends in *-e* in the masculine and feminine singular forms, the ending changes to *-i* in the plural. These adjectives follow the noun they modify. None of them is capitalized in Italian.

MASCULINE		FEMININE	
SINGULAR	PLURAL	SINGULAR	PLURAL
italiano	*italiani*	*italiana*	*italiane*
spagnolo	*spagnoli*	*spagnola*	*spagnole*
francese	*francesi*	*francese*	*francesi*
inglese	*inglesi*	*inglese*	*inglesi*

*il ragazzo **messicano***	the Mexican boy
*la ragazza **messicana***	the Mexican girl
*l'uomo **norvegese***	the Norwegian man
*la donna **norvegese***	the Norwegian woman

CONTINUED ON PAGE 46 ▶

5. Adjectives ending in *-io* in the singular change *-io* to *-i* in the plural.

il libro **vecchio**	the old book
i libri **vecchi**	the old books

6. A few adjectives are invariable and have only one form for both genders and numbers. Examples follow.

pari	even
dispari	odd

7. Some adjectives ending in *-co* or *-go* in the masculine singular have a masculine plural ending in *-ci* or *-gi.* The feminine singular ending *-ca* changes to *-che* in the plural.

pacifico	*pacifi**ci***	peaceable
pacifica	*pacifi**che***	

   Other adjectives ending in *-co* or *-go* add *h* in the masculine plural too.

bianco	*bian**chi***	white
bianca	*bian**che***	
largo	*lar**ghi***	big
larga	*lar**ghe***	

8. The adjectives of colors that derive from nouns are invariable.

rosa	pink	*Dov'è il vestito rosa?*	Where is the pink dress?
viola	purple	*Il muro della sua camera è viola.*	The wall in her room is purple.
blu	blue	*Lui ha una giacca blu.*	He has a blue jacket.

9. Some indefinite adjectives are invariable and modify only singular nouns.

ogni	every	*ogni settimana*	every week
qualche	some	*qualche nuvola*	a few clouds
qualsiasi	any	*qualsiasi penna*	any pen

10. Adjectives ending in a stressed vowel are invariable.

indù	Hindu
bantù	Bantu

11. A few adjectives drop their final vowel when they precede a noun.

	BEFORE THE NOUN	AFTER THE NOUN	EXAMPLES
MASCULINE SINGULAR	*buon*		*un buon ragazzo, un buon amico*
FEMININE SINGULAR	*buona*		*una buona ragazza*
	buon'		*una buon'amica*
MASCULINE AND	*grand'*	*grande*	*un grand'uomo, un uomo grande*
FEMININE SINGULAR	*gran*	*grande*	*una gran casa, una casa grande*
MASCULINE SINGULAR	*questo*		*questo libro*
	quest'		*quest'uomo*
FEMININE SINGULAR	*questa*		*questa macchina*
	quest'		*a quest'ora*
MASCULINE SINGULAR	*san*		*San Giuseppe*
	sant'	*santo*	*un sant'uomo, un uomo santo*

CONTINUED ON PAGE 47 ▶

The adjective *grande* becomes *gran* before most singular nouns of either gender. Its meaning then becomes "great" rather than "big."

12. The adjective *bello* ("beautiful, handsome, nice") and *quello* ("that") also have shortened forms that are similar to those of the definite articles.

	BEFORE A CONSONANT	BEFORE A VOWEL	BEFORE **Z** OR **S** + CONSONANT
MASCULINE SINGULAR	*bel giorno* beautiful day	*bell'uomo* handsome man	*bello studente* nice student
MASCULINE PLURAL	*bei capelli* beautiful hair	*begli occhi* beautiful eyes	*begli studenti* nice students
FEMININE SINGULAR	*bella macchina* beautiful car	*bell'amica* beautiful friend	
FEMININE PLURAL	*belle case* beautiful homes	*belle amiche* beautiful friends	
MASCULINE SINGULAR	*quel ragazzo* that boy	*quell'uomo* that man	*quello scalino* that step
MASCULINE PLURAL	*quei signori* those gentlemen	*quegli uomini* those men	*quegli studenti* those students
FEMININE SINGULAR	*quella strada* that road	*quell'oca* that goose	
FEMININE PLURAL	*quelle case* those homes	*quelle amiche* those friends	

Note that *bello* retains its full form when it follows the noun it modifies or the verb *essere*.

Un ragazzo bello non è sempre *interessante.*	A handsome boy is not always interesting.

WORD ORDER Normally, a descriptive adjective in Italian follows the noun it modifies. First, you say what you are talking about (for example, *una casa*), then you describe it (for example, *una casa bianca*).

Some adjectives, however, can be placed either before or after the noun. If an adjective is meant literally, it tends to follow the noun; if its meaning is figurative, it precedes the noun.

*un **grand'**uomo*	a great man
*un uomo **grande***	a tall man
*un'**antica** chiesa*	a former church
*una chiesa **antica***	an old church
*un **povero** uomo*	a poor man
*un uomo **povero***	a man with no money
*una **vecchia** amica*	an old friend
*un'amica **vecchia***	a friend who is old
*una **cara** amica*	a dear friend
*una giacca **cara***	an expensive jacket

When two descriptive adjectives appear together, the one most closely associated with the noun comes first.

l'arte italiana moderna	modern Italian art

English Comparison of adjectives

Definition   The three degrees of comparison are positive, comparative, and superlative.

Forms   English forms comparisons in the following ways.

1. Regular comparisons add -er and -est to short adjectives, sometimes with a minor change in spelling.

   short ~ shorter ~ shortest
   pretty ~ prettier ~ prettiest

2. Longer adjectives are compared by using *more* and *most*, or the negatives *less* and *least*.

   *determined ~ **more** determined ~ **most** determined*
   *obvious ~ **less** obvious ~ **least** obvious*

3. Some adjectives have irregular comparisons.

   good ~ better ~ best
   bad ~ worse ~ worst

4. Adjectives that cannot be compared include absolutes, which are by definition super-lative. Uniqueness and perfection cannot be brought to a higher degree.

   unique
   perfect

5. When a comparison is made, several words may introduce the second element: *than, in,* and *of all.*

   COMPARATIVE   *He is taller **than** I (am).*
   SUPERLATIVE   *He is the tallest boy **in** the class. He is the tallest **of all** my students.*

If an adjective is already in the comparative, *more* is not added. Greater contrast may be expressed by words like *much.*

   ***much** smaller*
   ***much** more difficult*

Forms   Italian forms comparisons in the following ways.

1. Regular Italian adjectives form the comparative with *più* ("more"), *tanto* ("as" in the sense of equal), or *meno* ("less") plus the adjective.

    *grande ~ **più** grande ~ **tanto** grande ~ **meno** grande*

2. Superlatives are formed with the definite article plus the comparative (for example, *il più grande* and *la meno piccola*).

    The adjective remains in the same position, whether it is positive, comparative, or superlative.

    *È una casa **grande**.*
    *È una casa **più grande**.*
    *È **la** casa **più grande** del villaggio. È **la più grande**.*

3. The most common irregular comparisons are the following.

*buono ~ **meglio** ~ **il migliore***	better ~ the best
*cattivo ~ **peggio** ~ **il peggiore***	worse ~ the worst
*grande ~ **maggiore** (OR **più grande**) ~ **il maggiore***	greater, bigger ~ the greatest
*piccolo ~ **minore** (OR **più piccolo**) ~ **il minore***	smaller ~ the smallest

4. Adjectives that cannot be compared include absolute adjectives, which are by definition superlative.

    unico
    perfetto

    Since uniqueness and perfection cannot be brought to a higher degree, *il/la/i/le più* cannot be used with them.

5. When a comparison is made between two elements, *di* or *che* is used to link them.

COMPARATIVE	*Giovanna è più grande **di** Maria.*
COMPARATIVE	*Giovanna è più bella **che** intelligente.*
SUPERLATIVE	*Maria è la più bella **della** sua famiglia.*

    Più... di and *meno... di* are used to compare one quality shared by two people or things. When the comparison is between two qualities possessed by a single subject, *che* is used instead of *di*.

 QUICK CHECK

COMPARATIVE CONSTRUCTION WITH (1) *gli uomini,* **(2)** *le donne,* **AND (3)** *sono grandi*

NOUN 1	+ VERB	+ COMPARATIVE	+ ADJECTIVE	+ *di/quanto*	+ NOUN 2
Gli uomini	*sono*	*più/meno*	*grandi*	*delle*	*donne.*
Gli uomini	*sono*	*tanto*	*grandi*	*quanto*	*le donne.*

SUPERLATIVE CONSTRUCTION WITH (1) *Giovanna,* **(2)** *la classe,* **AND (3)** *è più brava*

NOUN 1	+ VERB	+ SUPERLATIVE	+ ADJECTIVE	+ *di*	+ NOUN 2
Giovanna	*è*	*la più*	*brava*	*della*	*classe.*

Following are the key elements in comparative and superlative constructions.

1. Word order (see the **Quick Check** above)
2. Verb (agreement with the subject)
3. Adjective (agreement with the noun, noun phrase, or pronoun it describes)

English Proper adjectives

Definition   A proper adjective is a descriptive adjective formed from a proper noun (see page 12).

NOUN	ADJECTIVE
Rome	*Roman*
Shakespeare	*Shakespearean*

Forms   In English, both proper nouns and their adjectives are capitalized. Sometimes, their forms are indistinguishable.

NOUN	ADJECTIVE
the Italian	*the Italian people*

English Limiting adjectives

Definition   A limiting adjective does not add to your knowledge of a noun; instead, it directs you toward the right one by limiting the choices. The following examples show the types of limiting adjectives.

DEMONSTRATIVE	***this*** *chapter* (not another one)
POSSESSIVE	***his*** *book* (not hers)
INTERROGATIVE	***whose*** *coat?* (its specific owner)
INDEFINITE	***some*** *people* (but not others)
ORDINAL NUMBER	*the* ***second*** *lesson* (not the first)

Each of these types of limiting adjectives are discussed separately.

English Demonstrative adjectives

Definition   Demonstrative adjectives point out which of a group is/are the one(s) that you are referring to.

Forms   These adjectives have the same forms as the demonstrative pronouns (see page 36) and distinguish in the same way between near and far and between singular and plural.

	SINGULAR	PLURAL
NEAR	*this*	*these*
FAR	*that*	*those*

There is no agreement in person, gender, or case. The demonstrative adjective precedes its noun.

*****This*** *woman is talking to* ***that*** *man.*
*****These*** *little boys hate* ***those*** *dogs.*

 Proper adjectives

Forms In Italian, proper adjectives are formed from proper nouns, but they are not capitalized.

NOUN	ADJECTIVE
i Romani	*la gente romana*

 Limiting adjectives

See the discussion on the opposite page.

 Demonstrative adjectives

Forms A demonstrative adjective agrees with the noun it modifies in gender and number.

MASCULINE		FEMININE		
SINGULAR	PLURAL	SINGULAR	PLURAL	ENGLISH EQUIVALENT
questo	*questi*	*questa*	*queste*	this/these
quel, quello	*quei, quegli*	*quella*	*quelle*	that/those

Uses The near/far distinction made in English does not arise in Italian unless there is a possibility of confusion. Then, *qui* or *là* is added to the *questo/questa* or *quello/quella* phrase, respectively.

Questa casa qui è molto grande.   This house (over here) is really big.
Quella macchina là è vecchia.   That car (over there) is old.

 **Possessive adjectives**

Definition Possessive adjectives modify a noun by telling to whom or what it belongs.

Forms These adjectives indicate the person, number, and gender (in the third-person singular) of the *possessor*.

	SINGULAR	PLURAL
FIRST PERSON	*my*	*our*
SECOND PERSON	*your*	*your*
THIRD PERSON	*his, her, its, one's*	*their*

The adjectives do not tell anything about the person or thing that is possessed.

> ***Mr. Pellegrini's*** *son* → ***his*** *son* (third-person singular masculine)
> ***Mrs. Pellegrini's*** *son* → ***her*** *son* (third-person singular feminine)
> ***the Pellegrinis'*** *son* → ***their*** *son* (third-person plural)

Uses The possessive adjective is always used with the noun.

> ***my*** *mother*
> ***our*** *child*
> ***your*** *turn*

If the noun is omitted, a possessive pronoun must be used (for example, *mine, ours,* or *yours*) (see page 26).

 Possessive adjectives

Definition Italian possessives are adjectives, so they agree in gender and number with the noun they modify, *not* with the possessor.

Forms Italian possessive adjectives have the following forms.

	MASCULINE		FEMININE		ENGLISH EQUIVALENT
	SINGULAR	PLURAL	SINGULAR	PLURAL	
SINGULAR					
FIRST PERSON	*il mio*	*i miei*	*la mia*	*le mie*	my
SECOND PERSON	*il tuo*	*i tuoi*	*la tua*	*le tue*	your (sing.)
THIRD PERSON	*il suo*	*i suoi*	*la sua*	*le sue*	his, her, its
PLURAL					
FIRST PERSON	*il nostro*	*i nostri*	*la nostra*	*le nostre*	our
SECOND PERSON	*il vostro*	*i vostri*	*la vostra*	*le vostre*	your (pl.)
THIRD PERSON	*il loro*	*i loro*	*la loro*	*le loro*	their

This is quite different from English. *Il suo cappotto* can mean either "his coat" or "her coat." The masculine form *il suo* is used, because *cappotto* is masculine. For instance, Mary can say the following.

*Ecco **il mio** cappotto, **la mia** sciarpa e **i miei** guanti.*	Here are my coat, my scarf, and my gloves.

The possessive adjectives do not indicate Mary's gender, but they do indicate the genders and numbers of the three items that she possesses.

Possessive adjectives in Italian are normally preceded by a definite article. The definite article is not used, however, when the noun refers to a family member and is singular and unmodified.

***Mio fratello** si chiama Franco.*	My brother's name is Frank.
***Suo padre** viaggia molto.*	Her father travels a lot.

If the noun refers to more than one relative, or if the possessive adjective *il/la loro* ("their") is used, or if the noun is modified by another adjective, the definite article is always used.

***I nostri zii** sono molto anziani.*	Our uncles are very old.

Several idiomatic phrases in Italian do not take the definite article with the possessive adjective; in these phrases, the possessive adjective is placed after the noun.

casa mia, casa tua, etc.	my house, your house, etc.
è colpa mia, è colpa tua, etc.	it is my fault, it is your fault, etc.
piacere mio	my pleasure

English Interrogative adjectives

Definition   Interrogative adjectives ask a question about limitation.

Forms   These adjectives have case in English.

1. Subject and object cases: *which? what?*

2. Possessive case: *whose?*

These forms are invariable.

Uses   Interrogative adjectives are used

1. to ask a question.

SUBJECT	***What*** *assignment is for today?*
OBJECT	***Which*** *class do you have at 10 o'clock?*
POSSESSIVE	***Whose*** *coat is this?*

2. in an exclamation.

What *a pretty house!*
What *a job!*

 Interrogative adjectives

Forms In Italian, the interrogative adjective is inflected for gender and number. It agrees with the noun it modifies.

| MASCULINE | | FEMININE | | |
SINGULAR	PLURAL	SINGULAR	PLURAL	ENGLISH EQUIVALENT
che?	*che?*	*che?*	*che?*	what?
quale?	*quali?*	*quale?*	*quali?*	which? what?
quanto?	*quanti?*	*quanta?*	*quante?*	how much? how many?

As can be seen from this chart, the adjective *che?* has only one form and therefore does not distinguish between singular and plural or between genders. These adjectives present little difficulty for the learner of Italian as long as they appear directly before the noun. However, when they are separated by the verb, it is sometimes more difficult for English speakers to recognize them as adjectives.

While the forms of the adjective *quale?* distinguish between singular and plural, the same forms are used for both genders.

The form of *quanto?* reflects both gender and number.

Uses Interrogative adjectives are used

1. to ask a question.

Quanti *libri hai?*	How many books do you have?
Che *ora è?*	What time is it?
Che *compito abbiamo per domani?*	What homework do we have for tomorrow?
Qual'*è il giornale d'oggi?*	Which one is today's newspaper?

2. in an exclamation.

| **Che** *bella casa hai!* | What a beautiful house you have! |

 Indefinite adjectives

Definition Indefinite adjectives refer to nouns or pronouns that are not defined more specifically.

> **Some** students learn fast.
> **Any** girl will tell you.
> **Both** lectures are at 10 o'clock.
> **Each/Every** class has its value.
> I want **another** pen.
> **Such** behavior is terrible.

Forms These adjectives are invariable, that is, they do not change their form. Some, however, may be used only with singular nouns (for example, *each, every, another*), some only with plural nouns (for example, *both, other*), and some with either singular or plural nouns (for example, *some*: *some coffee, some people*).

 Other limiting adjectives

Ordinal numbers

These numbers indicate the order in which things come. *One, two*, and *three* (and all numbers ending in *one, two*, and *three*, except *eleven, twelve*, and *thirteen*) have irregular ordinals.

> *first, second, third*

All other ordinal numbers are formed by adding *-th*.

> *fourth, ninth, sixteenth*

Determiners

Determiners are often classified as adjectives (see page 16).

 Other adjectival forms

Many other kinds of words—even though they are not adjectives themselves—may be used as adjectives (that is, to describe a noun or pronoun).

NOUN	a **conference** room
PRESENT PARTICIPLE	**running** water
PAST PARTICIPLE	the **closed** windows
PREPOSITIONAL PHRASE	the poster **on the wall**
RELATIVE CLAUSE	the coat **that I bought**
INFINITIVE	I wonder what **to do**.
ADVERBIAL PHRASE	The students come **from all around**.

Italian Indefinite adjectives

Definition Italian indefinite adjectives are similar to those in English.

Forms An indefinite adjective agrees with its noun in gender and number, just as descriptive adjectives do.

Alcuni studenti imparano rapidamente.	Some students learn quickly.
Vorrei un'altra penna.	I would like another pen.
Ogni essere umano è degno di rispetto.	Every human being deserves respect.
Qualche donna te lo dirà.	Some woman will tell you.
Tutto il giornale è pieno di brutte notizie.	The whole newspaper is full of bad news.

The singular *tutto* means "the whole." The plural *tutti/tutte* means "all the . . .". Both forms are followed by the definite article.

*Ogni sera preparo **tutto il** programma per il giorno dopo.*	Each evening, I prepare the whole schedule for the following day.
*Ho comprato **tutte le** riviste italiane che ho trovato.*	I bought all the Italian magazines I found.

Italian Other limiting adjectives

Ordinal numbers

Ordinal numbers are essentially vocabulary items in Italian and need to be learned as such. They agree in gender and number with the noun they modify.

primo presidente
prima attrice
quinto piano
decima lezione

Determiners

See page 17.

Italian Other adjectival forms

NOUN PHRASE	*la sala **delle conferenze***
PRESENT PARTICIPLE	*l'acqua **corrente***
PAST PARTICIPLE	*le finestre **chiuse***
PREPOSITIONAL PHRASE	*l'orologio **da muro***
RELATIVE CLAUSE	*il cappotto **che comprai***
INFINITIVE	*Non so che **fare**.*
ADVERBIAL PHRASE	*Gli studenti vengono **da tutte le parti**.*

Adverbs

Definition See page 7.

Forms Most English adverbs formed from descriptive adjectives add *-ly* to the adjective.

> *active ~ actively*
> *slow ~ slowly*

1. Like adjectives, adverbs may be inflected to show comparison.

POSITIVE	COMPARATIVE	SUPERLATIVE
actively	*more actively*	*most actively*
actively	*less actively*	*least actively*

The comparative is used to show the similarity or difference between how two people or things do something, or the degree of difference in qualifying an adjective or adverb. The superlative compares more than two people or things. There must also be a word to link the two points of comparison.

POSITIVE	*I walk **slowly**.*
COMPARATIVE	*John walks **more slowly than** I do.*
SUPERLATIVE	*Monica walks **the most slowly of** all.*

2. Like adjectives, some adverbs not ending in *-ly* may take *-er* and *-est* in comparisons.

> *He runs fast, but I run **faster**.*
> *Mary runs the **fastest** of all.*

3. Some adverbs form their comparison irregularly.

POSITIVE	COMPARATIVE	SUPERLATIVE
well	*better*	*best*
badly	*worse*	*worst*

Uses English adverbs are used in the following ways.

1. Adverbs answer the questions *how, when, where,* or *how much* about a verb, an adjective, or another adverb. Sometimes, a phrase takes the place of a single adverb.

> ***Yesterday*** he came **here** and **very** **quickly** told the story.
> WHEN   WHERE   HOW MUCH HOW

> ***This morning*** he went **there** **by car**.
> WHEN   WHERE HOW

CONTINUED ON PAGE 62 ▶

Forms   Most Italian adverbs formed from descriptive adjectives add -*mente* to the feminine form of the adjective. Most of these are adverbs of manner.

> *attiva* → **attivamente**
> *lenta* → **lentamente**

1. Adverbs, unlike adjectives, have only one form.

2. Some of the most common Italian adverbs do not end in -*mente* and must be learned as vocabulary items.

> *andare* **forte**   *to go fast*
> *parlare* **chiaro**   *to speak clearly*

3. Like adjectives, adverbs may be inflected to show comparison.

POSITIVE	COMPARATIVE	SUPERLATIVE
attivamente	*più attivamente*	*il più attivamente*
	tanto attivamente quanto	
	così attivamente come	
	meno attivamente	*il meno attivamente*

The words used to link the two elements being compared are the same as for adjectives. (See the **Quick Check** on page 49.)

POSITIVE	*Giovanni legge* **rapidamente**.
COMPARATIVE	*Giovanni legge* **più rapidamente di** *Pietro.*
SUPERLATIVE	*Giovanni cammina* **il più lentamente di** *tutti.*

Two adverbs—meaning "well" and "badly"—form their comparisons irregularly.

POSITIVE	COMPARATIVE	SUPERLATIVE
bene	*meglio*	*il meglio*
male	*peggio*	*il peggio*

Another pair of adverbs that form their comparisons irregularly mean "much" and "(a) little."

molto	*di più*	*il più*
poco	*meno*	*il meno*

4. To make comparisons using verbs, *tanto come* is used after the verb.

> *Francesco non parla* **tanto come**   Francesco doesn't talk as much as
>   *suo padre.*   his father does.

Uses   Italian adverbs are used in the following ways.

1. See the English uses on the opposite page.

> **Ieri** *è venuto* **qui** *e*   **molto**   **in fretta** *ha raccontato la storia.*
> WHEN   WHERE HOW MUCH HOW

CONTINUED ON PAGE 63 ▶

2. **Negatives**. Some adverbs make a sentence negative. These include words like *not, nowhere,* and *never.* In standard English, two negative words in one sentence express a positive, not a negative, idea.

> *He doesn't have **no** friends, but he has **too few**.*

The first clause used alone and intended as a negative is not standard English. Not only are negative adverbs included here, but negative nouns and adjectives as well.

3. **Questions**. Another group of adverbs introduces questions: *when? where? how?* and *why?* The majority of adverbs answer these questions with respect to the verb, but the interrogative words themselves are adverbs too.

> ***When** does he arrive?*
> ***How** do you know that?*

Many adverbs can also be used as subordinating conjunctions in English (see page 66).

> *We are going to the movies **when** we finish our work.*

Adjectives vs. adverbs

To choose the correct word, it is essential to ask yourself the following questions.

1. Am I *describing someone/something*? → adjective

2. Am I *describing how/when/where/why something is done*? → adverb

> *The **poem** is **good**, and the poet **reads** it **well**.*
>   NOUN   ADJECTIVE   VERB   ADVERB

> *The **play** is **bad**, and it's **badly**   **performed**.*
>   NOUN ADJECTIVE   ADVERB VERB

This is especially important for verbs of mental or emotional state and for sensory verbs, which can be followed by either an adjective or an adverb. One of the most common examples is the following.

> *I feel **bad**.* (= I am sick/unhappy/etc.)
> *I feel **badly**.* (= My hands are not sensitive.)

2. **Negatives**

  a. The negative word *non* in Italian is an adverb and may come before

   • a conjugated verb.

   Non *parlo inglese.*   I don't speak English.

   • *avere, essere,* and *stare* when they are used as auxiliary verbs in compound tenses.

   Non *ho visto la maestra.*   I didn't see the teacher.
   Non *stiamo lavorando molto.*   We're not working much.

   • an object pronoun that precedes a verb.

   Non *mi piace quello.*   I don't like that.

  b. Other common negative adverbs that accompany verbs follow.

non... mai	never
non... più	no longer
non... per niente	not at all
non... nessuno	no one
non... né... né	neither . . . nor

   Non *vedo* **nessuno.**   I don't see anybody.
   Non *ho* **né** *tempo* **né** *denaro.*   I have neither time nor money.
   Non *parlo* **né** *a Giovanni* **né** *a Pietro.*   I speak neither to John nor to Peter.
   Non *leggo* **né** *parlo giapponese.*   I neither read nor speak Japanese.

   Mai, più, per niente, and *nessuno* may precede the verb; in this case, *non* is omitted. If these words follow the verb, *non* must precede it.

   Nessuno *mi ama.*   No one loves me.
       OR **Non** *mi ama* **nessuno.**
   Mai *parlo inglese in Italia.*   I never speak English in Italy.
       OR **Non** *parlo* **mai** *l'inglese in Italia.*

3. **Questions**

   Quando *venite? Veniamo domani.*   When are you coming? We're coming tomorrow.

   Dove *sono le forbici? Sono nel cassetto.*   Where are the scissors? They're in the drawer.

   Come *ti chiami? Mi chiamo Giovanni.*   What's your name? My name is John.

Many adverbs can also be used as subordinating conjunctions in Italian (see page 67).

   Mi riposo **quando** *finisco il mio lavoro.*   I'll rest when I finish my work.

Adjectives vs. adverbs

La **poesia** *è* **bella***, e il poeta l'***ha letta bene***.*
  NOUN   ADJECTIVE   VERB   ADVERB

Il **libro** *è* **noioso***, e tutti lo* **leggono malvolentieri***.*
  NOUN   ADJECTIVE   VERB   ADVERB

Conjunctions

English Introducing conjunctions

Definition See page 7.

Forms Conjunctions are function words; they are invariable.

Types All conjunctions are linking words, but the linked elements and their relationship with each other determine which of the three principal types a conjunction belongs to: coordinating, subordinating, or adverbial.

Uses English conjunctions are used as follows.

1. A **coordinating conjunction** links two equal elements that have the same grammatical construction. The two elements may be single words, phrases, or entire clauses.

NOUNS	*John **and** Mary*
INFINITIVES	*to be **or** not to be*
INDEPENDENT CLAUSES	*We came, **but** he wasn't home.*

   Correlatives, which occur in pairs, are a subgroup of coordinating conjunctions.

   ***Both** John **and** Mary are in the class.*
   ***Either** we go now **or** we don't go at all.*

2. A **subordinating conjunction** joins unequal elements. One element is subordinated to the other. The conjunction introduces the subordinate clause (the one that cannot stand alone as a sentence).

CONTRAST	***Although** he wants to be on time, he is late.*
TIME	*We speak Italian **when** our friends come over.*
CAUSE	***Because** this course is easy, we all get "A"s.*

   Notice that the main idea of the sentence is in the main (independent) clause. The subordinate clause tells about the time, way, cause, or conditions involved and may show a contrast. Notice also that the main clause need not come first. You could reverse the order of the clauses in each example above without changing the meaning of the sentence.

   There is also a subgroup of correlative subordinating conjunctions (for example, *if . . . then* and *so . . . that*).

   *This course is **so** hard **that** many students have complained.*

3. An **adverbial conjunction** is sometimes called a "conjunctive adverb." Grammarians are not sure whether they are really adverbs or conjunctions. Words and phrases like *therefore, perhaps, also, for example, as a result,* and *in other words* fall into this category.

Uses Italian conjunctions are used as follows.

1. Coordinating conjunctions

NOUNS	*Giovanni e Maria*
INFINITIVES	*essere o non essere*
INDEPENDENT CLAUSES	*Noi siamo venuti, **ma** non era a casa.*

Correlative conjunctions are a subgroup of coordinating conjunctions.

***Sia** Giovanni **sia** Maria sono nella classe.*
***O** andiamo adesso **o** non andiamo più.*

2. Subordinating conjunctions

CONTRAST	***Benché** lui voglia essere puntuale, è in ritardo.*
TIME	*Parliamo italiano **quando** vengono i nostri amici.*
CAUSE	***Dato che** questo corso è facile, abbiamo tutti "A".*

Correlative conjunctions are a subgroup of subordinating conjunctions.

*Questo corso è **così** difficile **che** molti studenti si sono lamentati.*

3. Adverbial conjunctions

dunque, può essere, per esempio, etc.

Interjections

English | Introducing interjections

Definition   See page 7.

Forms   Interjections are normally invariable exclamations.

Uses   As an exclamation, an interjection is often merely a sound meant to convey emotion (for example, *ow!*). It has no grammatical connection with the other words in the sentence and is set off by commas.

Italian Introducing interjections

Interjections present no problems for the learner of Italian; they are simply vocabulary items followed by an exclamation point. Following are some common ones.

Ahi!
Ahimè!
Aiuto!
Beh!
Boh!
Ohi!
Suvvia!

Prepositions

English Introducing prepositions

Prepositions in any language are very tricky words. Most of them have basic meanings, but when they are used in phrasal verb constructions, that meaning can change. A phrasal verb is a combination of a verb plus (usually) a preposition that has a meaning different from the combined meanings of the words. You may think, for example, that you know what *up* means, but consider the following sentence.

> First he cut the tree **down**, then he cut it **up**.

People learning English would be confused by that sentence, and it is not an isolated example. Take the case of a friend telephoning John's house early in the morning and asking for him. John's wife might reply as follows.

> He'll be **down** as soon as he's **up**.

In other words, after learning a preposition and its basic meanings, one must be alert to how it is used in phrasal verb constructions. Often, the meanings of a single preposition will spread over several pages of a dictionary.

Definition See page 7.

Forms A preposition is a function word; it is invariable. It can be a single word or a group of words (for example, *by* and *in spite of*).

CONTINUED ON PAGE 76 ▶

 Introducing prepositions

Forms An Italian preposition can be one or several words; examples are *con* ("with"), *vicino a* ("near"), and *lontano da* ("far from").

A one-to-one equivalence between English and Italian prepositions is rare. They are capricious in both languages.

Prepositions are invariable, except when they combine with the definitive article. In Italian, five of the most commonly used prepositions—*a* ("at, to"), *da* ("from, by"), *di* ("of, about, from"), *in* ("in, into"), and *su* ("on")—combine with the definite article to form a contraction.

a + il → al	*Luigi va al cinema.*	Louis goes to the movies.
da + lo → dallo	*I giocatori ritornano dallo stadio.*	The players return from the stadium.
di + la → della	*La casa della mia amica è bella.*	My friend's house is beautiful.
in + il → nel	*I libri sono nel cassetto.*	The books are in the drawer.
su + il → sul	*L'uccellino è sul tetto.*	The bird is on the roof.

Note that the prepositions *di* and *in* change to *de* and *ne*, respectively, when they combine with the definite article.

The following chart shows the most common prepositional contractions.

	MASCULINE SINGULAR	MASCULINE PLURAL	FEMININE SINGULAR	FEMININE PLURAL
a	*a + il → al* *a + lo → allo*	*a + i → ai* *a + gli → agli*	*a + la → alla*	*a + le → alle*
da	*da + il → dal* *da + lo → dallo*	*da + i → dai* *da + gli → dagli*	*da + la → dalla*	*da + le → dalle*
di	*di + il → del* *di + lo → dello*	*di + i → dei* *di + gli → degli*	*di + la → della*	*di + le → delle*
in	*in + il → nel* *in + lo → nello*	*in + i → nei* *in + gli → negli*	*in + la → nella*	*in + le → nelle*
su	*su + il → sul* *su + lo → sullo*	*su + i → sui* *su + gli → sugli*	*su + la → sulla*	*su + le → sulle*

Other prepositions, such as *con* ("with"), *per* ("for"), and *tra* and *fra* ("among, between") do not combine with the definite article.

CONTINUED ON PAGE 77 ▶

Uses A preposition links a noun or pronoun (its object) to other words in the sentence and shows the object's relationship to them. In formal English, a preposition is followed immediately by its object.

> *to* the store
> *about* the subject

In informal English, a preposition is often placed at the end of the clause or sentence, especially in questions and relative clauses.

> *What* is she waiting *for?*
>   INSTEAD OF *For what* is she waiting?
> *This is the one* **that** he is referring **to**.
>   INSTEAD OF *This is the one* **to which** he is referring.

Introducing prepositions (continued)

Uses   In English, many verbs are followed by prepositions that change the meaning of the verb. Italian often distinguishes these meanings with different verbs.

> *cercare*   to look **for**
> *guardare*   to look **at**
> *indagare*   to look **into**

At times, an English verb may be followed by a preposition when it has an object noun, but not when used alone. In Italian, such verbs are never followed by a preposition.

> ITALIAN   *Ascolta la radio! Ascoltalo! Ascolta!*
> ENGLISH   Listen to the radio! Listen to it! Listen!

In English, a preposition comes before its object in formal speech and writing, but not always in informal speech. In Italian (and many other languages), it must always do so.

> INFORMAL ENGLISH   Who are you going to the movies **with**?
> FORMAL ENGLISH   **With** whom are you going to the movies?
> ITALIAN (INFORMAL OR FORMAL)   *Con chi vai al cinema?*

Because the same English word may be translated by more than one Italian word, it is necessary to know the word's function in a sentence. For example, the English word *before* may be

1. a conjunction followed by a subject and verb ("**before** someone did something") = *prima di.*

2. a preposition expressing location ("**before** the bank") = *davanti a.*

3. a preposition expressing time ("**before** 3 o'clock") = *prima di.*

Special problems with prepositions

1. It is important to distinguish between Italian prepositions that express the same word in English.

> *sopra a*   on
> *in cima a*   on (top of)

2. Geographical names require specific prepositions to express "to," "in," and "from."

	to/in		*from*	
COUNTRIES	*in*	*Io vado **in** Italia.*	*da* + definite article	*Vengo **dal** Brasile.*
CONTINENTS	*in*	*Io vado **in** Africa.*	*da* + definite article	*Veniamo **dal** Sud America.*
STATES*	*in*	*Vivono **in** California.*	*da* + definite article	*Viene **dalla** California.*
PROVINCES	*in*	*Andate **in** Toscana.*	*da* + definite article	*Venite **dalla** Toscana.*
CITIES†	*a*	*Andiamo **a** Roma.*	*da*	*Viene **da** Roma.*

---

*The states of the United States are masculine except for a few well-known ones: *la California, la Florida, la Pennsylvania, la Carolina del Nord, la Carolina del Sud,* and *l'Arizona.*
†If the name of the city contains a definite article, the article remains.
> *il Cairo*
> *La Paz*

CONTINUED ON PAGE 78 ▶

3. Conjugated verbs are often followed by infinitives. If two verbs are used to express a single thought, the *first* determines whether a preposition (and which one) is used to introduce the infinitive that follows. There can even be more than two infinitives in a string.

Following is a list of verbs and the prepositions they take when followed by an infinitive. In idiomatic expressions, the English preposition may or may not be equivalent to the Italian preposition.

andare a	**Vado a** *vederlo domani.*	I'm **going to** see him tomorrow.
cominciare a	*La giovane* **cominciò a** *ridere.*	The young woman **began to** laugh.
imparare a	*Io* **ho imparato a** *guidare la macchina questa estate.*	I **learned to** drive the car this summer.
insegnare a	*L'insegnante mi* **ha insegnato a** *parlare bene l'italiano.*	My teacher **taught** me **to** speak Italian well.
mandare a	*Mia madre mi* **ha mandato a** *comprare la verdure.*	My mother **sent** me **to** buy some vegetables.
venire a	**Vengo a** *vederlo domani.*	I'm **coming to** see him tomorrow.
fingere di	*I bambini* **fingevano di** *dormire.*	The children **were pretending to** be asleep.
promettere di	*Lui* **ha promesso di** *venire.*	He **promised to** come.
sperare di	**Speriamo di** *vederti presto.*	We **hope to** see you soon.

A compound verb usually requires the same preposition as the basic verb.

Io **ricomincio a** *studiare l'italiano.*	I'm starting to study Italian again.
Mi **riprometto di** *studiare.*	I intend to study.

4. Some adjectives are followed by a preposition before an infinitive, just as some verbs are. The Italian and English prepositions in these constructions often do not "match."

ultimo a	*Maria è sempre l'***ultima a** *finire.*	Mary is always the **last one to** finish.
lento a	*Io sono molto* **lenta a** *imparare la chimica.*	I am very **slow at** learning chemistry.

5. Verbs may also require a particular preposition before a noun or a pronoun object.

dare su	*La finestra* **dà sulla** *piazza.*	The window **looks out on** the square.
ridere di	**Ha riso di** *tutti noi.*	He **laughed at** all of us.

10

Verbs

Introducing verbs

Definition	See page 7.	
Forms	English has fewer inflected verb forms than any continental European language. Many English verbs have only four forms (for example, *talk, talks, talked, talking*); some have five forms (for example, *sing, sings, sang, sung, singing*).	

In some systems of grammar, it is said that, technically, English has only two tenses—present and past—and that other temporal concepts are expressed by periphrastic verbal constructions. This means that English uses helping verbs and other expressions to convey temporal differences. Verbs are presented here in a more traditional way, because it will help you see the parallels between English and Italian constructions. Following are the principal parts of an English verb.

INFINITIVE	SIMPLE PAST	PAST PARTICIPLE	PRESENT PARTICIPLE
talk	*talked*	*talked*	*talking*
sing	*sang*	*sung*	*singing*

Some words used to identify verb forms are **conjugation**, **tense**, **voice**, **transitive**, **intransitive**, and **mood**.

Conjugation

This word has two meanings.

1. In Latin and in modern Romance languages, verbs are classified into groups, or conjugations, by their infinitive endings. English and German have only *regular* and *irregular* (sometimes called *weak* and *strong*) verbs. Weak verbs take a regular ending to form the past (for example, *talk ~ talked* and *follow ~ followed*). Strong verbs often change the vowel in their past forms, and some past forms may look completely different from their infinitives (for example, *sing ~ sang* and *go ~ went*).

2. Conjugation also refers to a list, by person, of each form in a given tense. Latin has six forms in each tense. Following are the present-tense forms of *amare* ("to love").

	SINGULAR	PLURAL
FIRST PERSON	*amo* I love	*amamus* we love
SECOND PERSON	*amas* you (singular) love	*amatis* you (plural) love
THIRD PERSON	*amat* he/she loves	*amant* they love

Since each form is different, it is not necessary to use a pronoun subject: The verb ending tells you who the subject is. The same is true for Spanish and Italian today.

In English, verbs can be conjugated but usually are not, because there is only one inflected ending: -s is added to the third-person singular of the simple present tense.

	SINGULAR	PLURAL
FIRST PERSON	*I speak*	*we speak*
SECOND PERSON	*you speak*	*you speak*
THIRD PERSON	*he/she speaks*	*they speak*

A noun or pronoun is required with every verb form, because otherwise it would not be known who or what the subject is.

Tense

This word comes from Latin *tempus* via French *temps,* meaning "time." The tense tells *when* something happened, *how long* it lasted, and whether it is *completed.*

Voice

English has two voices: active and passive. **Active voice** means that the subject is or is doing something.

> *Mary is happy.*
> *Mary reads the newspaper.*

In these examples, *Mary* is the subject.

Passive voice means that the subject is acted on by an agent. The verb tells what happens to the subject.

> *The newspaper is read by Mary.*

In this example, *newspaper* is the subject.

Transitive verbs

These verbs require an object to express a complete meaning.

> *Mr. White surprised a burglar.*

In this example, the verb *surprised* is transitive, because it takes an object, *burglar.* If we omitted the object, the sentence would not make sense; it would be incomplete.

Intransitive verbs

These verbs do not require an object.

> *Paul sat down.*

Here, the verb *sat* is intransitive, because it has no object; *down* is an adverb.

English has many verbs that can be either transitive or intransitive.

Peter	***eats***	*dinner*	*at 7 o'clock.*
The butcher	***weighs***	*the meat.*	
SUBJECT	TRANSITIVE VERB	DIRECT OBJECT	

Peter	***eats***	*at 7 o'clock.*
The butcher	***weighs***	*a lot.*
SUBJECT	INTRANSITIVE VERB	

Mood

This grammatical concept indicates the mood, or attitude, of the speaker. Is the speaker stating a fact? Giving an order? Offering a possibility that has not happened yet? Making a recommendation? Three moods are used to express these ideas: indicative, imperative, and subjunctive. The indicative is by far the most common mood. The other two are used in special circumstances and are discussed later in this chapter.

English Introducing questions

Forms   There are four ways to ask a question in English.

1. Place a question mark after a statement and raise the pitch of your voice at the end of the statement when saying it aloud.

   Anne is here already?
   That's Mark's idea?

2. Add a "tag," repeating the verb or auxiliary verb as a negative question. In English, the specific tag depends on the subject and the verb.

   *Peter is happy, **isn't he?***
   *Anna finished studying, **didn't she?***

3. Invert the subject and an auxiliary or modal verb or the verb *to be*.

PRESENT	***Do you** have any brothers?*
PRESENT PROGRESSIVE	***Is Peter** buying his books?*
PRESENT	***Does Peter** buy his books?*
PRESENT PERFECT	***Has Peter** bought his books?*
PRESENT	***May I** see you this evening?*
PRESENT	***Is Robert** here today?*

4. Use an interrogative word.

   ***Where** is the library?*
   ***When** does the library open?*

Italian Introducing questions

Forms   There are four ways to ask a question in Italian.

1. Place a question mark after a statement and raise the pitch of your voice at the end of the statement when saying it aloud. This method is usually limited to conversations (oral and written).

   Anna è già qui?
   È un'idea di Marco?

2. Place *non è vero?*, *vero?*, or *no?* after a statement with which you expect the hearer or reader to agree.

   Pietro è contento, **non è vero?**
   Anna ha finito di studiare, **vero?**

3. Invert the subject and verb. If an object noun or adverb is present, the subject is placed at the end of the question. You do not need an auxiliary verb to form a question, as you do in English.

Suona il piano Giovanni?	Does John play the piano?
Canta bene Maria?	Does Mary sing well?

   Inversion is not used, however, with *io*.

4. Begin the sentence with an interrogative word.

Dove *è Maria?*	Where is Mary?
Dove *sono le scarpe?*	Where are the shoes?
Quando *venite?*	When are you coming?
A che ora *apre la biblioteca?*	When does the library open?

These rules apply to a simple tense (one in which the verb is expressed by one word). In compound tenses (those that use two or more words to form the verb), the auxiliary verb is treated in the same way as in simple tenses.

Pietro ha comprato il libro?	Did Peter buy the book?
Con chi hai parlato?	With whom did you speak?

Word order

WITH NEGATIVES   A single negative word precedes the conjugated verb. If there is a double negative, the first negative word precedes the conjugated verb and the second immediately follows it.

Tu **non** *hai* **mai** *visto Parigi?*	Have you never been to Paris?

WITH PRONOUN OBJECTS   As with statements, pronoun objects go directly before the verb in questions. A negative word precedes the object pronoun.

Non lo *avete visto?*	Didn't you see him?

WITH OTHER KINDS OF QUESTIONS   When you use intonation, *è vero?*, or *non è vero?* to ask a question, the word order is the same as for a statement. See the examples above.

Introducing verbals

Definition   Verbals are forms of the verb that are not finite, that is, do not agree with a subject and do not function as the predicate of a sentence. There are five types of verbals: present infinitive, past infinitive, gerund, present participle, and past participle.

 Present infinitives

Definition   The present infinitive is the basic form of the verb, as it appears in a dictionary.

Forms   The infinitive is often identified by the word *to* preceding it. However, *to* is omitted in many infinitive constructions, especially after verbs like *can* and *let*. Compare the following sentences, both of which contain the infinitive *swim*.

> *I know how **to swim**.*
> *I can **swim**.*

Uses   In addition to completing the verb, as in the above examples, an infinitive may serve as the subject or object of a sentence, as an adjective, or as an adverb.

SUBJECT	***To err** is human.*
OBJECT	*He hopes **to come** soon.*
ADJECTIVE	*English is the subject **to study**.*
ADVERB	***To tell** the truth, I don't believe her.*

Infinitives may also have their own direct objects and other modifiers.

> *I am able **to do** that   easily.*
>   DIRECT OBJECT ADVERB

Past infinitives

Forms   The past infinitive is formed with the present infinitive of the auxiliary verb plus the past participle of the main verb.

> *to go* (present infinitive) → *to have gone* (past infinitive)

Uses   The past infinitive is used in the same ways as the present infinitive.

> ***To have quit** is terrible.*

Italian Present infinitives

Forms   Italian verbs are grouped in three conjugations by the ending of their infinitives: *-are*, *-ere*, and *-ire*.

Uses   The Italian infinitive may be used in several ways.

SUBJECT/COMPLEMENT	***Vedere** è **credere***.
OBJECT	*Lui spera di **arrivare** presto.*
ADJECTIVE	*L'inglese è la materia da **studiare**.*
ADVERB	*A **dire** il vero, io non la credo.*

Infinitives may have objects (either nouns or pronouns) and be negated or otherwise modified.

DIRECT OBJECT	*Vado a vedere **il museo**.*
DIRECT AND INDIRECT OBJECT	*Vado a leggere **la rivista a mio zio**.*
	*Vado a legger**gliela**.*
ADVERB	*Voglio capire **meglio** la fisica.*
NEGATIVE	*Preferisco **non arrivare** troppo tardi.*

Italian Past infinitives

Forms   Past infinitives are formed as in English, with the present infinitive of the auxiliary (*avere* or *essere*, depending on the verb) plus the past participle of the main verb.

PRESENT INFINITIVE	PAST INFINITIVE
studiare	*avere studiato*
vendere	*avere venduto*
dormire	*avere dormito*
andare	*essere andato*

Uses   The past infinitive is used like the present infinitive, but it expresses past time.

***Dopo aver mangiato**, è andato a dormire.*	After eating (having eaten), he went to sleep. OR After he ate, he went to sleep.

The past infinitive must be used with the preposition *dopo*.

***Dopo aver mangiato**, è partito.*	After eating (having eaten), he left. OR After he ate, he left.

English · Gerunds

Definition Gerunds are often called verbal nouns.

Forms The English gerund is formed by adding *-ing* to the infinitive form of the verb.

> *sing → singing*
> *run → running*
> *bite → biting*

Uses Gerunds have the same functions as other nouns (see page 10).

> SUBJECT **Walking** *is good for you.*
> OBJECT *I like* **singing**.

Gerunds may also have objects and modifiers.

> **Making** *money* *quickly is many people's goal.*
> DIRECT OBJECT ADVERB

English · Participles

Definition Participles are verbal adjectives that constitute the third and fourth principal parts of a verb.

Forms English has two participles.

1. **Present participles** (the fourth principal part) end in *-ing*.

> *singing*
> *talking*
> *managing*

2. **Past participles** (the third principal part) end in *-ed* or *-n* for regular verbs.

> *tried*
> *gathered*
> *concentrated*
> *given*

To determine the past participle of an irregular verb, say, "Today I go; yesterday I went; I have gone; I am going." The form used after "I have" is the past participle. In the dictionary, the principal parts are given for every irregular verb.

CONTINUED ON PAGE 88 ▶

 Gerunds

Italian has no gerund; the infinitive is used as the verbal noun (see examples in the Present infinitives section (page 85)).

Guadagnare soldi rapidamente, è il fine di molte persone.

 Participles

Forms   Italian has two participles.

1. **Present participles** are invariable, that is, they do not change for gender or number.

   Most verbs whose infinitives end in *-are* add *-ando* to the stem of the infinitive (after dropping *-are*).

parlare	**parlando**

   Verbs whose infinitive ends in *-ere* or *-ire* add *-endo* to the stem of the infinitive (after dropping *-ere* and *-ire*).

vendere	**vendendo**
sentire	**sentendo**

   Some common verbs have irregular present participles.

bere	**bevendo**
dire	**dicendo**
fare	**facendo**

2. **Past participles** have different endings for the different conjugations. Drop the infinitive ending *-are, -ere,* or *-ire* and add *-ato, -uto,* or *-ito* to the stem of the verb.

parlare	**parlato**
vedere	**veduto**
sentire	**sentito**

CONTINUED ON PAGE 89 ▶

Uses   The two types of participles have the same basic uses.

1. As part of a compound verb (one consisting of two or more words)

   PRESENT PROGRESSIVE   *He **is talking**.*
   PAST PERFECT   *They **have given**.*

2. As an adjective

   a ***talking*** *doll*
   a ***proven*** *fact*

3. In an absolute phrase modifying a noun

   Walking *along the street, he met Robin.*
   Seen *from the front, the building was even more imposing.*

   In the two examples above, *he is* walking and *the building* was *seen*.

A number of Italian verbs have irregular past participles; following are some of the most common.

accendere	**acceso**
aprire	**aperto**
bere	**bevuto**
chiudere	**chiuso**
cuocere	**cotto**
dire	**detto**
essere	**stato**
fare	**fatto**
leggere	**letto**
mettere	**messo**
morire	**morto**
nascere	**nato**
porre	**posto**
prendere	**preso**
scrivere	**scritto**
spegnere	**spento**

Uses   A **present participle** is used

1. with *stare* to form the progressive tenses.

*Maria **sta cantando**.*	Mary is singing.
*Giovanni **stava spiegando**.*	John was explaining.

2. in a subordinate clause whose subject is the same as that of the main clause.

***Conoscendo** molto bene la città,*	Knowing the city very well,
Elena ha fatto da guida.	Elena served as a guide.

Some nouns and adjectives with endings resembling that of the present participle were once verbals. These may be used as nouns or adjectives.

cantante	singer
ambulante	walking
seguente	following

A **past participle** is used

1. with *avere* and *essere* to form the perfect tenses.

*Edoardo **ha finito** il suo lavoro.*	Edward finished his work.
*Maria **ebbe terminato** il lavoro.*	Mary had finished the job.
*Giovanni **è ritornato** dal lavoro tardi.*	John returned late from work.

2. as an adjective.

*il libro **aperto***	the open book
*la Terra **Promessa***	the Promised Land
*il Mar **Morto***	the Dead Sea
*un fatto **provato***	a proven fact

3. as a noun.

*il primo **venuto***	the first (person) to arrive
*i **sopravvissuti***	the survivors

Indicative mood

The verbs on pages 90–113 are all in the indicative mood. It is the one used for stating facts and for making assertions as though they were facts.

English Present tense

Definition The present tense is defined by its uses (see page 92).

Forms There are three present tenses in English: simple present, present progressive, and present emphatic.

1. **Simple present**. There is only one inflected form in the simple present: the third-person singular, which adds -s to the basic verb form.

	SINGULAR	PLURAL
FIRST PERSON	I sing	we sing
SECOND PERSON	you sing	you sing
THIRD PERSON	he/she sings	they sing

2. **Present progressive**. This tense is formed with the present tense of to be plus the present participle.

	SINGULAR	PLURAL
FIRST PERSON	I am singing	we are singing
SECOND PERSON	you are singing	you are singing
THIRD PERSON	he/she is singing	they are singing

3. **Present emphatic**. This tense is formed with the present tense of to do plus the infinitive.

	SINGULAR	PLURAL
FIRST PERSON	I do sing	we do sing
SECOND PERSON	you do sing	you do sing
THIRD PERSON	he/she does sing	they do sing

CONTINUED ON PAGE 92 ▶

~~Italian~~ Present tense

Forms   Unlike English, Italian has only two forms of the present tense: the simple present and the present progressive. The simple present form *parlo* may be translated as "I speak," "I am speaking," or "I do speak." The present progressive is used only to stress the fact that the action is going on now: *sto parlando* ("I am speaking (at this very moment)").

1. **Regular *-are* verbs**. To form the simple present tense, drop the infinitive ending (*-are*) and add *-o, -i, -a; -iamo, ate, -ano*.

	SINGULAR	PLURAL
FIRST PERSON	*parlo*	*parliamo*
SECOND PERSON	*parli*	*parlate*
THIRD PERSON	*parla*	*parlano*

   To form the present progressive tense, use the present tense of *stare* and the present participle.

	SINGULAR	PLURAL
FIRST PERSON	*sto parlando*	*stiamo parlando*
SECOND PERSON	*stai parlando*	*state parlando*
THIRD PERSON	*sta parlando*	*stanno parlando*

   The present participles of *essere* and *stare* are never used in the progressive tenses.

2. **Regular *-ere* verbs**. Drop the infinitive ending (*-ere*) and add *o, -i, -e; -iamo, -ete, -ono*.

	SINGULAR	PLURAL
FIRST PERSON	*vedo*	*vediamo*
SECOND PERSON	*vedi*	*vedete*
THIRD PERSON	*vede*	*vedono*

3. **Regular *-ire* verbs** (*sentire* type). Drop the infinitive ending (*-ire*) and add *o, -i, -e; -iamo, -ite, -ono*.

	SINGULAR	PLURAL
FIRST PERSON	*sento*	*sentiamo*
SECOND PERSON	*senti*	*sentite*
THIRD PERSON	*sente*	*sentono*

4. **Regular *-ire* verbs** (*finire/capire* type). Drop the infinitive ending (*-ire*), add *-isc* to the three singular and the third-person plural stems, and add the regular *-ire* endings.

	SINGULAR	PLURAL
FIRST PERSON	*finisco*	*finiamo*
SECOND PERSON	*finisci*	*finite*
THIRD PERSON	*finisce*	*finiscono*

CONTINUED ON PAGE 93 ▶

Uses   The **simple present** is used for

1. an action or state occurring in the present.

   *They **speak** Chinese.*

2. an habitual action that is still true.

   *I always **study** in the evening.*

3. existing facts and eternal truths.

   *Paris **is** the capital of France.*
   *I **think**, therefore I **am**.* (René Descartes)

The **present progressive** is used to

1. stress the continuing nature of the verb's action in either a statement or a question.

   *I **am** still **trying**!*
   ***Are** you **going** to the library now?*

2. make a future action seem more immediate.

   *We **are reading** this book next week.*
   *I **am going** to the show tomorrow.*

The **present emphatic** is used to

1. add emphasis or contradict.

   *I **do want** to do well.*
   *They **do** not **do** that!*

2. form questions or negative statements.

   ***Do** you **go** to the lake in the summer?*
   *I **do** not **know** what you are talking about.*

5. **Stem-changing verbs.** A few Italian verbs change their present tense stems.

andare	*vado, vai, va; andiamo, andate, vanno*
avere	*ho, hai, ha; abbiamo, avete, hanno*
essere	*sono, sei, è; siamo, siete, sono*
fare	*faccio, fai, fa; facciamo, fate, fanno*
morire	*muoio, muori, muore; moriamo, morite, muoiono*
potere	*posso, puoi, può; possiamo, potete, possono*
volere	*voglio, vuoi, vuole; vogliamo, volete, vogliono*

6. **Verbs with orthographic (spelling) changes.** Verbs in this group require a spelling change in the written language to reflect the need to keep the same final consonant sound throughout the present tense.

   a. Verbs ending in *-care* and *-gare* add *h* before endings with *e* or *i* to maintain the hard sound of the *c* or *g*.

giocare	*gioco, gio**chi**, gioca; gio**chiamo**, giocate, giocano*
pagare	*pago, pa**ghi**, paga; pa**ghiamo**, pagate, pagano*

   b. Verbs ending in *-ciare* and *-giare* drop the *i* before endings with *e* or *i*.

mangiare	*mangio, man**gi** (NOT mangii), mangia; man**gi**amo, mangiate, mangiano*

   c. Verbs ending in *-iare* drop the *i* of the stem if it is not in the accented syllable.

studiare	*studio, stud**i** (NOT studii), studia; studiamo, studiate, studiano*
avviare	*avvio, avv**ii** (NOT avvi), avvia; avviamo, avviate, avviano*

Uses

1. All of the uses listed for the three present tenses in English are filled by this one tense in Italian. To emphasize that one is in the act of doing something, the present progressive is used.

2. Italian also uses the present tense with *da* to express an action that began in the past and is still going on in the present.

***Aspetto** la lettera **da** due settimane.*	I have been waiting for the letter for two weeks. (I began waiting two weeks ago, and I am still waiting.)
***Studio** l'italiano **da** due mesi.*	I have been studying Italian for two months (and I am still studying it).

English Past tense

Definition The past tense describes actions or states in the past.

Forms There are three past tenses, each corresponding to one of the three present tenses discussed in the previous section. (For perfect tenses, see pages 102–111.)

1. The **simple past** is the second principal part of the verb (see page 80). It is not inflected; all of the forms are the same. The simple past of weak verbs ends in -ed (for example, *talked* and *wished*). Strong verbs have irregular past forms.

	SINGULAR	PLURAL
FIRST PERSON	*I sang*	*we sang*
SECOND PERSON	*you sang*	*you sang*
THIRD PERSON	*he/she sang*	*they sang*

2. The **past progressive** is formed with the simple past of the verb *to be* plus the present participle of the main verb.

	SINGULAR	PLURAL
FIRST PERSON	*I was singing*	*we were singing*
SECOND PERSON	*you were singing*	*you were singing*
THIRD PERSON	*he/she was singing*	*they were singing*

3. The **past emphatic** is formed with the simple past of the verb *to do* plus the infinitive.

	SINGULAR	PLURAL
FIRST PERSON	*I did sing*	*we did sing*
SECOND PERSON	*you did sing*	*you did sing*
THIRD PERSON	*he/she did sing*	*they did sing*

Uses The three past tenses closely parallel the three present tenses in usage, except that the action takes place in the past. The simple past states a fact, the past progressive emphasizes the duration or continuation of an action at a given moment in the past, and the past emphatic stresses a statement and is used to form negatives and questions.

Other past forms

Other expressions provide special past meanings.

1. Immediate past action: *to have just* plus the past participle

   Mary **has just arrived** this minute.

2. Habitual past action: *used to* or *would* plus the infinitive

   I **used to go** to the movies every week.
   For a long time, I **would see** them every day.

3. Repeated past action: *kept (on)* plus the present participle

   He **kept (on) doing** it.

Forms The imperfect tense is formed with the verb stem plus special endings. The stem is formed by dropping the -*re* of the infinitive and adding the same endings to all three conjugations.

parlare	*vedere*	*sentire*
parlavo	*vedevo*	*sentivo*
parlavi	*vedevi*	*sentivi*
parlava	*vedeva*	*sentiva*
parlavamo	*vedevamo*	*sentivamo*
parlavate	*vedevate*	*sentivate*
parlavano	*vedevano*	*sentivano*

Essere is the only verb that is irregular in the imperfect. The stem is *er-*, and the endings are regular.

> *essere*   ero, eri, era; eravamo, eravate, erano

The **imperfect progressive** tense is formed with the imperfect of *stare* plus the present participle.

parlare	*vedere*	*sentire*
stavo parlando	*stavo vedendo*	*stavo sentendo*
stavi parlando	*stavi vedendo*	*stavi sentendo*
stava parlando	*stava vedendo*	*stava sentendo*
stavamo parlando	*stavamo vedendo*	*stavamo sentendo*
stavate parlando	*stavate vedendo*	*stavate sentendo*
stavano parlando	*stavano vedendo*	*stavano sentendo*

Uses The Italian imperfect tense is used for

1. description: What you are describing is more important than the action or the background against which the action takes place. See the English "used to" construction.

2. habitual action: See the English "used to / would" construction.

3. duration, or continuing action: See the English past progressive.

4. repeated action: See the English "kept (on)" construction.

The imperfect tense is used on the basis of these principles, not on a one-to-one correspondence with English tenses or idioms. The imperfect is used many times when the simple past tense is used in English.

DESCRIPTION	**Era** *lunedì e* **pioveva**.	It was Monday, and it was raining.
HABITUAL ACTION/ DESCRIPTION	**Andavo** *in quella scuola quando* **ero** *piccolo.*	I went to that school when I was a child.
DURATION	**Leggeva** *tutte le sere.*	He read every evening.

Other past tenses

Other tenses that describe past time are the preterite (see page 97); the present perfect (see page 103); the past perfect (see page 107); the preterite perfect (see page 107); the future perfect (see page 109); the perfect conditional (see page 111); the imperfect subjunctive (see page 120); the present perfect subjunctive (see page 121); and the past perfect subjunctive (see page 121).

CONTINUED ON PAGE 96 ▶

Compare the imperfect with the preterite tense, which is used for completed actions.

PRETERITE VS. IMPERFECT

PRETERITE	IMPERFECT
Event happened once	Event happened often (repeated/habitual)
Finished and completed event	Continuing, unfinished event
Series of distinct events	Description
Maria lesse il libro in due settimane.	*Maria leggeva sempre fino a tardi.*
Il telefono suonò...	*mentre Maria dormiva.*
Luigi andò a Roma, cercò un albergo	*Maria era una ragazza italiana che*
e vi stette per due giorni.	*viveva a Roma, ma passava le vacanze*
	in Svizzera.

Other past forms

For "used to" or "would" (in the sense of "used to") + an infinitive, use the imperfect tense of the verb.

*Quando ero giovane, **andavo** al cinema tutte le domeniche.*

When I was young, I used to / would go to the movies every Sunday.

 Preterite tense

Forms The preterite tense is formed by dropping the infinitive endings and adding special endings to the stem.

parlare	vendere	sentire
parlai	vendei	sentii
parlasti	vendesti	sentisti
parlò	vendé	sentì
parlammo	vendemmo	sentimmo
parlaste	vendeste	sentiste
parlarono	venderono	sentirono

A number of verbs have irregular preterite forms. Following are the most common.

bere	bevvi, bevesti, bevve; bevemmo, beveste, bevvero
chiedere	chiesi, chiedesti, chiese; chiedemmo, chiedeste, chiesero
chiudere	chiusi, chiudesti, chiuse; chiudemmo, chiudeste, chiusero
conoscere	conobbi, conoscesti, conobbe; conoscemmo, conosceste, conobbero
dire	dissi, dicesti, disse; dicemmo, diceste, dissero
dovere	dovetti, dovesti, dovette; dovemmo, doveste, dovettero
fare	feci, facesti, fece; facemmo, faceste, fecero
leggere	lessi, leggesti, lesse; leggemmo, leggeste, lessero
nascere	nacqui, nascesti, nacque; nascemmo, nasceste, nacquero
sapere	seppi, sapesti, seppe; sapemmo, sapeste, seppero
scendere	scesi, scendesti, scese; scendemmo, scendeste, scesero
spegnere	spensi, spegnesti, spense; spegnemmo, spegneste, spensero
stare	stetti, stesti, stette; stemmo, steste, stettero
tradurre	tradussi, traducesti, tradusse; traducemmo, traduceste, tradussero
vedere	vidi, vedesti, vide; vedemmo, vedeste, videro
venire	venni, venisti, venne; venimmo, veniste, vennero
vincere	vinsi, vincesti, vinse; vincemmo, vinceste, vinsero
vivere	vissi, vivesti, visse; vivemmo, viveste, vissero
volere	volli, volesti, volle; volemmo, voleste, vollero

Verbs ending in *-durre* (for example, *condurre* and *produrre*) follow the preterite pattern of *tradurre*.

Uses The preterite is approximately equivalent to the simple past in English. It expresses a completed action in the past. (See the chart on page 96 for its uses contrasted with those of the imperfect.)

English Future tense

Definition The future tense describes events that have not yet taken place.

Forms There are only two tenses for future time: the future and the future progressive. Both are compound tenses, that is, they require more than one word to form them.

1. The **future tense** is formed by using the auxiliary verb *will* plus the infinitive of the main verb.

	SINGULAR	PLURAL
FIRST PERSON	*I will sing*	*we will sing*
SECOND PERSON	*you will sing*	*you will sing*
THIRD PERSON	*he/she will sing*	*they will sing*

2. The **future progressive tense** is formed with the future of *to be* plus the present participle. It therefore requires three words.

	SINGULAR	PLURAL
FIRST PERSON	*I will be singing*	*we will be singing*
SECOND PERSON	*you will be singing*	*you will be singing*
THIRD PERSON	*he/she will be singing*	*they will be singing*

NOTES

1. There are no irregular future tense forms in English.

2. *Will* is often contracted to *'ll*.

> *We'**ll** do it tomorrow.*
> *You'**ll** be studying that next week.*

Uses The distinction between the future and future progressive tenses is the same as that between the corresponding present tenses (see page 92). They are used

1. to express an action or state that will happen or exist in the future.

2. in Type 1 conditional sentences, where the *if*-clause is in the present. (See the **Quick Check** on page 110.)

> *If you **study**, you **will succeed**.*

Other future forms

Another way to express future action is an idiomatic use of *to go* plus the infinitive of the main verb.

> *I **am going to sing** tomorrow.*

✎Italian✎ Future tense

Forms There is only one future tense in Italian. It is formed with a stem plus special endings. The stem is the full infinitive without the final *e*. In the first conjugation, the *a* of the infinitive ending changes to *e* in the future. The endings are *-ò, ai, -à; -emo, -ete, -anno.*

NOTES

1. The endings are the same for all verbs, even irregular ones. Any irregularities are in the stem.

2. There is an accent in the first- and third-person singular endings.

3. Future stems, both regular and irregular, always end in *r*.

parlare	*perdere*	*dormire*	*essere*	*stare*
parlerò	*perderò*	*dormirò*	*sarò*	*starò*
parlerai	*perderai*	*dormirai*	*sarai*	*starai*
parlerà	*perderà*	*dormirà*	*sarà*	*starà*
parleremo	*perderemo*	*dormiremo*	*saremo*	*staremo*
parlerete	*perderete*	*dormirete*	*sarete*	*starete*
parleranno	*perderanno*	*dormiranno*	*saranno*	*staranno*

4. A number of verbs have irregular stems in the future, even though their endings are regular. These stems are also used to form the conditional tense (see page 101).

andare	**andr-**	*porre*	**porr-**
avere	**avr-**	*sapere*	**sapr-**
bere	**berr-**	*tenere*	**terr-**
cadere	**cadr-**	*vedere*	**vedr-**
dovere	**dovr-**	*venire*	**verr-**
essere	**sar-**	*volere*	**vorr-**
fare	**far-**		

Uses The future tense in Italian is used

1. to express an action or state that will happen or exist.

   *Luisa **arriverà** in gennaio.*

2. in Type 1 conditional sentences, where the *se*-clause is in the present. (See the **Quick Check** on page 111.)

   *Se **studiate**, **riuscirete** bene.*

3. as a command for the future (like English).

   ***Discuterai** la tesi mercoledì.*   You will present your thesis on Wednesday.

4. to indicate possibility.

   *Chi **sarà**? **Sarà** tua sorella.*   I wonder who that is? It must be your sister.

5. to convey the future from a past perspective.

   *Domenica Giovanna ha detto: "Va bene, **verrò** da voi lunedì."*
   Martedì Roberto ha detto: "Giovanna ha detto che sarebbe venuta da noi lunedì."

   In the second sentence, *sarebbe venuta* is in the perfect conditional tense.

English Conditional tense

Definition
Many grammarians do not consider the conditional to be a true tense, but rather a mood. We consider it a tense here, however, since this analysis will make its parallels with Italian obvious.

Forms
The **conditional tense** is formed with the auxiliary verb *would* plus the infinitive of the main verb.

	SINGULAR	PLURAL
FIRST PERSON	*I would sing*	*we would sing*
SECOND PERSON	*you would sing*	*you would sing*
THIRD PERSON	*he/she would sing*	*they would sing*

The **conditional progressive tense** is formed with the conditional of the verb *to be* plus the present participle. It therefore requires three words.

	SINGULAR	PLURAL
FIRST PERSON	*I would be singing*	*we would be singing*
SECOND PERSON	*you would be singing*	*you would be singing*
THIRD PERSON	*he/she would be singing*	*they would be singing*

Would is often contracted to *'d.*

> *I'd go if you did.*

Uses
The conditional is used

1. in Type 2 conditional sentences (*If* CONDITION, *(then)* RESULT.). (See the **Quick Check** on page 110.)

> *If I were rich, (then) I **would go** to Europe every year.*

2. to convey the future from a past perspective.

FUTURE	*On Sunday, John said, "OK, I **will** see you on Monday."*
CONDITIONAL	*On Tuesday, Robert says, "John said that he **would** see us on Monday."*

Italian   Conditional tense

Definition In Italian, the conditional is often considered a mood rather than a tense, since it expresses speculation, not facts. This distinction, however, has no practical effect on its forms or uses.

Forms The conditional tense uses the same stem as the future for all regular and irregular verbs (see page 99). Add the conditional endings to the future stem: *-ei, -esti, -ebbe; -emmo, -este, -ebbero.*

parlare	*perdere*	*dormire*
parlerei	*perderei*	*dormirei*
parleresti	*perderesti*	*dormiresti*
parlerebbe	*perderebbe*	*dormirebbe*
parleremmo	*perderemmo*	*dormiremmo*
parlereste	*perdereste*	*dormireste*
parlerebbero	*perderebbero*	*dormirebbero*

Uses Like the English conditional, the conditional in Italian is used

1. in Type 2 conditional sentences (*Se* CONDITION [*imperfect subjunctive*], RESULT [*conditional*].). (See the **Quick Check** on page 111.)

   Se io fossi ricco, **andrei** *in Europa tutti gli anni.*

2. to convey the future from a past perspective.

   Paolo dice, "Bene, studierò domani."
   Andrea dice, "Paolo ha detto che **studierebbe** *domani."*

3. to express probability.

   Sarebbero *molto contenti.*

4. to make a polite request.

   Vorrei *un caffè, per favore.*

 ## Perfect (compound) tenses

Definition   The perfect tenses express

1. the time of the action or state.

2. the fact that it is completed.

"Perfect" in this sense comes from Latin *perfectus*, meaning "finished" or "completed." If something has been perfected, it needs no further work. "Perfect" here, then, does not mean "ideal."

Types   There are four perfect tenses corresponding to each of the tenses already discussed: present, past, future, and conditional.

 ## Present perfect tense

Forms   The present perfect tense is formed with the present tense of the verb *to have* plus the past participle of the main verb.

	SINGULAR	PLURAL
FIRST PERSON	*I have sung*	*we have sung*
SECOND PERSON	*you have sung*	*you have sung*
THIRD PERSON	*he/she has sung*	*they have sung*

Uses   This tense indicates that from the point of view of the present time, the action has been completed. Compare the following sentences.

*I **saw** that movie yesterday.*
*I **have seen** that movie.*

The first sentence, using *saw*, stresses a *past* action—what I did yesterday. The second stresses that I am currently experienced with that movie: I now know what it is about, that is, I *have* (present) *seen* (completed, finished with) that movie.

An idiomatic use of this tense is associated with the words *for* and *since*.

*I **have tried for** three hours to phone him.*
*I **have tried since** five o'clock to phone him.*

In the first sentence, the present perfect tense implies that there is a momentary lull, but the three hours of trying have lasted up to the present.

 Perfect (compound) tenses

Forms All perfect tenses in the active voice are formed with a single auxiliary and the past participle of the main verb. (See pages 87 and 89 for participle formation.)

Types In Italian, there is a perfect tense that corresponds to each of the simple (one-word) tenses. These perfect tenses are used much as their English counterparts.

 Present perfect tense

Forms The present perfect tense is formed with the present tense of the auxiliary verb plus the past participle of the main verb.

AUXILIARIES Italian, like German and French, has two possible auxiliary verbs. In fact, English had a second form at one time (*The hour **is** come*), but it is now considered obsolete.

Avere is used with a large majority of verbs. *Essere* is used

1. with a small group of verbs—all intransitive, all expressing motion or change. Verbs formed by adding a prefix to these verbs also use *essere* (for example, *divenire* and *rinvenire* (< *venire*)).

2. with verbs that are used reflexively or reciprocally.

*Noi **ci siamo incontrati** al ristorante.*	We met at the restaurant.
*Loro **si sono divertiti** al parco.*	They had fun at the park.

Avere is used with sentences that have a direct object (where the verb is transitive).

parlare	*vendere*	*finire*	*andare*
ho parlato	*ho venduto*	*ho finito*	*sono andato/andata*
hai parlato	*hai venduto*	*hai finito*	*sei andato/andata*
ha parlato	*ha venduto*	*ha finito*	*è andato/andata*
abbiamo parlato	*abbiamo venduto*	*abbiamo finito*	*siamo andati/andate*
avete parlato	*avete venduto*	*avete finito*	*siete andati/andate*
hanno parlato	*hanno venduto*	*hanno finito*	*sono andati/andate*

AGREEMENT OF THE PAST PARTICIPLE When a past participle is used as an adjective, it agrees with the noun it modifies, as expected.

l'italiano parlato	spoken Italian
oggetti perduti	lost and found

CONTINUED ON PAGE 105 ▶

 **Present perfect progressive tense**

Definition All progressive tenses emphasize duration, and all are conjugated with the auxiliary verb *to be* plus the present participle of the main verb.

Forms The present perfect progressive tense in English uses *to be* in the present perfect with the main verb expressed by its present participle.

	SINGULAR	PLURAL
FIRST PERSON	*I have been singing*	*we have been singing*
SECOND PERSON	*you have been singing*	*you have been singing*
THIRD PERSON	*he/she has been singing*	*they have been singing*

Uses Like other progressive tenses, the present perfect progressive tense emphasizes duration. Consider the following sentences.

> I **have tried** since five o'clock to phone him.
> I **have been trying** for three hours to phone him.

The second sentence stresses how long the three hours have seemed to me.

When used as part of a perfect tense, the past participle follows one of two rules for agreement.

1. The past participles of intransitive verbs conjugated with *essere* agree with the subject.

   *Lei **è morta**, noi **siamo venuti**.*   She died, and we came.

2. All other past participles agree with the direct object if it comes before the verb.

   *Questa è la casa che mi piace. **L'hanno**   This is the house I like. My friends*
   *   comprata** i miei amici.*   bought it.

 QUICK CHECK

The following rules apply to all perfect (compound) tenses, not just the present perfect.

USE OF THE CORRECT AUXILIARY	AGREEMENT OF THE PAST PARTICIPLE
essere: intransitive verbs of motion or change	Rule 1: agrees with the subject
essere: verbs used reflexively or reciprocally	Rule 1: agrees with the subject
avere: all other verbs	Rule 2: agrees with the direct object if the object comes before the verb

WORD ORDER The auxiliary verb—the one that is conjugated—typically fills the same position in the sentence that a simple-tense verb would hold, and the past participle is placed at the end.

 QUICK CHECK

Giovanni lo dice.	*Giovanni l'ha detto.*
Giovanni non lo dice.	*Giovanni non l'ha detto.*
Te lo dice?	*Te l'ha detto?*
Non glielo dice.	*Non gliel'ha detto.*

Uses   The present perfect in Italian refers to an action completed in the past; the imperfect is used for other situations.

Compare the present perfect with the preterite.

PRETERITE	PRESENT PERFECT
Action completed in the remote past	Action completed in the recent past
*Io **andai** a visitare il museo.*	*Ieri **sono andata** a visitare il museo.*
*Tu **venisti** dall'America.*	***Sei venuta** dall'America.*
*Noi **studiammo** la filosofia.*	*Noi **abbiamo studiato** la filosofia.*

The preterite is used more in southern Italy than in the northern part of the country.

 Past perfect (pluperfect) tense

Definition   The past perfect tense indicates that some action (or state) was completed before some other past action (or state).

Forms   The past perfect tense is formed with the simple past tense of the auxiliary verb *to have* plus the past participle of the main verb.

	SINGULAR	PLURAL
FIRST PERSON	*I had sung*	*we had sung*
SECOND PERSON	*you had sung*	*you had sung*
THIRD PERSON	*he/she had sung*	*they had sung*

These forms are often contracted to *I'd, you'd,* and so on.

*I'd **returned** the book before you asked for it.*

Uses   Think of the past time sequence in terms of "yesterday" (past) and "last week" (further in the past).

*Mary **had finished** her homework before I **began** to talk to her.*
    PAST PERFECT: last week   PAST: yesterday

 Past perfect progressive tense

Definition   This tense shares characteristics with others that have been introduced. It is

1. past (in terms of time).

2. perfect (in the sense of "completed").

3. progressive (with stress on duration).

Forms   The past perfect progressive tense is formed with the past perfect tense of the verb *to be* plus the present participle of the main verb.

	SINGULAR	PLURAL
FIRST PERSON	*I had been singing*	*we had been singing*
SECOND PERSON	*you had been singing*	*you had been singing*
THIRD PERSON	*he/she had been singing*	*they had been singing*

Uses   This tense expresses an action (or state) that had been continuing just before another past action (or state).

*I **had been waiting** for three weeks when the letter **arrived**.*

That is, the wait started three weeks before the letter arrived.

 # Past perfect (pluperfect) tense

Forms   The past perfect tense in Italian is formed with the imperfect tense of the auxiliary (*avere* or *essere*) plus the past participle of the main verb.

parlare	*andare*
avevo parlato	*ero andato/andata*
avevi parlato	*eri andato/andata*
aveva parlato	*era andato/andata*
avevamo parlato	*eravamo andati/andate*
avevate parlato	*eravate andati/andate*
avevano parlato	*erano andati/andate*

Uses   Just as in English, the past perfect tense in Italian refers to an action or state completed further in the past than some other past action or state.

*Maria **aveva finito** il suo lavoro, quindi **ho potuto** parlarle.*

PAST PERFECT: last week   PRESENT PERFECT: yesterday

 # Preterite perfect tense

Forms   The preterite perfect tense is formed with the preterite of the auxiliary *avere* plus the past participle of the verb.

parlare
ebbi parlato
avesti parlato
ebbe parlato
avemmo parlato
aveste parlato
ebbero parlato

Uses   The preterite perfect tense is now used primarily in literature. The forms are given here, because you may encounter this tense in reading. The meanings are the same as for the past perfect, which is used in everyday speech and writing.

English · Future perfect tense

Definition   This tense expresses an action that will be completed at some time in the future.

Forms   The future perfect tense is formed with the future tense of the auxiliary *to have* plus the past participle of the main verb.

	SINGULAR	PLURAL
FIRST PERSON	*I will have sung*	*we will have sung*
SECOND PERSON	*you will have sung*	*you will have sung*
THIRD PERSON	*he/she will have sung*	*they will have sung*

These forms are often contracted in speech to *I'll've, you'll've,* and so on.

Uses   This tense is used to express future completion.

> I **will have finished** the book before the professor **gives** an exam.
> FUTURE PERFECT   PRESENT

In the second clause, the present tense is used in English, even though the verb refers to an action in the future; the professor is not giving an exam now.

English · Future perfect progressive tense

Definition   This tense expresses an action or state that will be continued and then completed in the future.

Forms   The future perfect progressive tense is formed with the future perfect tense of the auxiliary *to be* plus the present participle of the main verb.

	SINGULAR	PLURAL
FIRST PERSON	*I will have been singing*	*we will have been singing*
SECOND PERSON	*you will have been singing*	*you will have been singing*
THIRD PERSON	*he/she will have been singing*	*they will have been singing*

Uses   This tense is used to emphasize the duration of an action whose beginning point is not specified but whose completion (at least provisionally) will be in the future.

> I **will have been studying** English for 16 years when I **graduate**.
> FUTURE PERFECT PROGRESSIVE   PRESENT

Although graduation is in the future, English uses the present tense. The sentence does not indicate when the speaker will graduate, nor when he or she began to study English. The important point is the relationship between the verbs in the two clauses; 16 years of study will be completed at the moment in the future when I graduate.

Italian Future perfect tense

Forms   The future perfect tense is formed with the auxiliary in the future tense plus the past participle of the main verb.

parlare	andare
avrò parlato	sarò andato/andata
avrai parlato	sarai andato/andata
avrà parlato	sarà andato/andata
avremo parlato	saremo andati/andate
avrete parlato	sarete andati/andate
avranno parlato	saranno andati/andate

Uses   The future perfect tense is used

1. as in English.

2. to express a future completed action in sentences with *quando, allorché,* and *dopo che,* even if English uses the present tense (see page 92).

*Quando voi verrete, io **avrò terminato** il mio lavoro.*	When you come (sometime in the future), I will have finished my work.
*Quando l'**avrete terminato**, ne parleremo.*	When you have finished it (sometime in the future), we will discuss it.

 Perfect conditional tense

Forms This tense is formed with the conditional tense of *to have* plus the past participle of the main verb.

	SINGULAR	PLURAL
FIRST PERSON	*I would have sung*	*we would have sung*
SECOND PERSON	*you would have sung*	*you would have sung*
THIRD PERSON	*he/she would have sung*	*they would have sung*

These forms are often contracted in speech to *I'd've, you'd've,* and so on.

> ***I'd've** come if I'd known.*

Uses This tense is used primarily in the result clauses of Type 3 conditional sentences (see the **Quick Check** below).

> *He **would have seen** the film if he **had known** that it was so good.*
> *We **would have come** if we   **had known** about it.*
>   PERFECT CONDITIONAL   PAST PERFECT

The *'d* in English can be a contraction of both *had* and *would*. This can cause some confusion unless the meaning of a sentence is analyzed.

> *If he**'d said** he needed it, **I'd have given** it to him.*
>   PLUPEFECT   PERFECT CONDITIONAL

 QUICK CHECK

THE THREE MOST COMMON TYPES OF CONDITIONAL SENTENCES IN ENGLISH

if-CLAUSE	RESULT CLAUSE	*if*-CLAUSE	RESULT CLAUSE
1. *If you **are** ready,*	*we **will** go.*	PRESENT	FUTURE
2. *If you **were** ready,*	*we **would** go.*	SUBJUNCTIVE	CONDITIONAL
3. *If you **had been** ready,*	*we **would have** gone.*	PLUPERFECT	PERFECT CONDITIONAL

 Perfect conditional progressive tense

Forms This tense is formed with the perfect conditional tense of the auxiliary *to be* plus the present participle of the main verb.

	SINGULAR	PLURAL
FIRST PERSON	*I would have been singing*	*we would have been singing*
SECOND PERSON	*you would have been singing*	*you would have been singing*
THIRD PERSON	*he/she would have been singing*	*they would have been singing*

Uses The perfect conditional progressive tense is used in the same way as the perfect conditional, except that the idea of duration is added.

> *I **would** not **have been sleeping** when you arrived, if I **had known** you were coming.*
>   PERFECT CONDITIONAL PROGRESSIVE   PAST PERFECT

 # Perfect conditional tense

Forms This tense is formed with the conditional of the auxiliary plus the past participle of the main verb.

parlare	andare
avrei parlato	sarei andato/andata
avresti parlato	saresti andato/andata
avrebbe parlato	sarebbe andato/andata
avremmo parlato	saremmo andati/andate
avreste parlato	sareste andati/andate
avrebbero parlato	sarebbero andati/andate

Uses In Italian, the perfect conditional tense is used, as in English, primarily for Type 3 conditional sentences (see the **Quick Check** below).

> *Lui **avrebbe visto** il film se **avesse saputo** che era così bello.*
>   PERFECT CONDITIONAL   PLUPERFECT SUBJUNCTIVE

 QUICK CHECK

THE THREE TYPES OF CONDITIONAL SENTENCES IN ITALIAN

se-CLAUSE	RESULT CLAUSE	*se*-CLAUSE	RESULT CLAUSE
1. *Se **sei** pronto,*	***andremo** al cinema.*	PRESENT	FUTURE
2. *Se tu **fossi** pronto,*	***andremmo** al cinema.*	IMPERFECT SUBJUNCTIVE	PRESENT CONDITIONAL
3. *Se tu **fossi stato** pronto, **saremmo andati** al cinema.*		PLUPERFECT SUBJUNCTIVE	PERFECT CONDITIONAL

English Passive voice

Definition The passive voice is used when the subject receives the action of the verb.

ACTIVE VOICE	**The dog**	*bit*	**Susie.**
	SUBJECT	ACTIVE VERB	DIRECT OBJECT
PASSIVE VOICE	**Susie**	*was bitten*	**by the dog.**
	SUBJECT	PASSIVE VERB	AGENT

Notice that the direct object of the active verb becomes the subject of the passive verb. The active verb's subject is placed after the passive verb in a prepositional phrase and is called the agent. It is not always expressed, as in the colloquial *John got caught*; for such a sentence, it is either not important or not known by whom or what John was caught.

Forms The passive voice is formed with *to be* or *to get* plus the past participle of the main verb.

Only transitive verbs (ones that have a direct object) can be made passive.

PRESENT	ACTIVE	*John **catches** the ball.*
	PASSIVE	*The ball **is caught** by John.*
PAST	ACTIVE	*The man **read** the book.*
	PASSIVE	*The book **was read** by the man.*
FUTURE	ACTIVE	*Mrs. Smith **will lead** the discussion.*
	PASSIVE	*The discussion **will be led** by Mrs. Smith.*
PERFECT CONDITIONAL	ACTIVE	*The class **would have finished** the job, but . . .*
	PASSIVE	*The job **would have been finished** by the class, but . . .*

All the perfect and progressive tenses of the passive voice are formed in the same way. Some forms can be very long and are seldom used; an example of the passive future perfect progressive follows.

*The work **will have been being done** at 3 P.M.*

Italian Passive voice

Forms The passive voice in Italian is formed with the verb *essere* (sometimes with the verb *stare*) plus the past participle of the main verb acting like an adjective, that is, agreeing with the subject in gender and number.

The passive voice is used in all tenses, including the subjunctive mood. In Italian, the agent in a passive construction is preceded by the preposition ***da***.

PRESENT	ACTIVE	*Maria **prende** la palla.*
	PASSIVE	*La palla **è presa** da Maria.*
PRESENT PERFECT	ACTIVE	*Lui **ha letto** il libro.*
	PASSIVE	*Il libro **è stato letto** da lui.*

In Italian, the passive voice in all tenses is formed with the appropriate tense of *essere* (or *stare*) plus the past participle of the main verb.

Uses Italians prefer the active voice to the passive. (English teachers often suggest using the passive voice as a way of improving one's writing, and authors sometimes even tend to use less vivid language when writing in the passive.) Compare the following English sentences.

PASSIVE	*Our receiver was tackled by their defensive end.*
ACTIVE	*Their defensive end slammed our receiver to the ground.*
PASSIVE	*This abstract was painted by Pablo Picasso.*
ACTIVE	*Pablo Picasso created this colorful abstract.*

If speakers of English are less than enthusiastic about the passive, the Italians actively dislike it. As a result, it is seldom used. There are a number of ways to avoid the passive voice in Italian.

1. Turn the sentence around.

   NOT *Il libro **fu letto** dalla classe.*
   BUT *La classe **lesse** il libro.*

2. Use the reflexive.

   NOT *Qui **è parlato** l'italiano.*
   BUT *Qui **si parla** l'italiano.*

English Imperative mood

Definition   The imperative mood is the mood used to give commands.

Forms   The forms of the English imperative are very similar to those of the present indicative, with a few exceptions.

The second-person imperative (both singular and plural) has only one form: *Sing!*

For the first-person plural, the auxiliary verb *let* is used.

> *Let's sing!*

For the third-person (singular and plural), the auxiliary verbs *let, have,* and *make* are used.

> *Let her sing!*
> *Have them come in!*
> *Make him stop!*

No subject is expressed in an imperative sentence.

IRREGULAR IMPERATIVES English has only one irregular imperative: for the verb *to be*. Compare the following sentences.

INDICATIVE	IMPERATIVE
You are good.	*Be good!*
We are quiet.	*Let's be quiet!*

Imperative mood

Forms   The imperative mood in Italian has three types of commands: the familiar (*tu* and *voi*), the formal (*Lei* and *Loro*), and the first-person plural (*noi*).

AFFIRMATIVE COMMANDS   These forms are similar to those of the present tense, except that the *tu* form of *-are* verbs ends in *-a* instead of *-i*.

	parlare	*scrivere*	*dormire*	*finire*
tu FORM	*parla!*	*scrivi!*	*dormi!*	*finisci!*
noi FORM	*parliamo!*	*scriviamo!*	*dormiamo!*	*finiamo!*
voi FORM	*parlate!*	*scrivete!*	*dormite!*	*finite!*

The first-person plural is typically a suggestion or an urgent request rather than a command.

NEGATIVE COMMANDS   To form the negative command, place *non* before the affirmative command for the *voi* form; for the *tu* form, place *non* before the infinitive.

	parlare	*scrivere*	*dormire*	*finire*
tu FORM	*non parlare!*	*non scrivere!*	*non dormire!*	*non finire!*
voi FORM	*non finite!*	*non scrivete!*	*non dormite!*	*non finite!*

FORMAL COMMANDS   For the third-person formal command, the subjunctive mood is used (see pages 117–118). The notion "I want" is understood.

	parlare	*scrivere*	*dormire*	*finire*
Lei FORM	*parli!*	*scriva!*	*dorma!*	*finisca!*
Loro FORM	*parlino!*	*scrivano!*	*dormano!*	*finiscano!*

Che entri!	Let her enter! (= I want her to enter.)
Che entrino!	Let them enter! (= I want them to enter.)

IRREGULAR IMPERATIVES   A few Italian verbs have irregular forms in the imperative mood.

	tu FORM	*voi* FORM
andare	*va'* OR *vai*	
avere	*abbi*	*abbiate*
dare	*da'* OR *dai*	
dire	*di'*	
essere	*sii*	*siate*
stare	*sta'* OR *stai*	

WORD ORDER   In affirmative commands, pronoun objects follow the verb and are attached to it. The indirect object always precedes the direct object (see page 25).

*Dam**melo**!*	Give it to me!
*Dim**melo**!*	Tell (it to) me!

The negative formal command is formed by placing *non* before the affirmative command form.

***Non** parli!*	Don't speak!
***Non** scrivano!*	Don't write!

Objects and reflexive pronouns precede the *Lei* and *Loro* forms.

***Mi** scriva!*	Write me!
***Si** sveglino!*	Wake up!

English Subjunctive mood

Definition   The subjunctive is the mood that expresses what may be true.

Forms   The **present subjunctive** (or the auxiliary verb in a compound tense) has the same form for all persons: the basic (infinitive) form of the verb. It is different from the indicative only for

1. the third-person singular.

    that he take
    that she have

2. the verb *to be.*

    PRESENT   *that I be, that he be*
    PAST   *that I were, that she were*

Uses   The subjunctive is rarely used in English. For that reason, it tends to be disregarded except in certain fixed expressions. Nevertheless, it does have some specific uses that are important in formal English.

1. In contrary-to-fact conditions

    *If I **were** you . . .*
    *"If this **be** madness, yet there is method in it." (Hamlet)*

2. After verbs like *wish, suppose, insist, urge, demand, ask, recommend,* and *suggest*

    *I wish that he **were** able to come.*
    *They insisted that we **be** present.*
    *I recommend that she **learn** the subjunctive.*

3. After some impersonal expressions, such as *it is necessary* and *it is important*

    *It is necessary that Mary **see** its importance.*
    *It is important that he **avoid** errors.*

4. In certain fixed expressions

    *So **be** it!*
    *Long **live** the Queen!*
    *Heaven **forbid**!*
    *Far **be** it from me to suggest that!*

    Most of these fixed expressions express a third-person imperative; the idea "I wish that" is implied, but not expressed.

    Except for the fixed expressions, English speakers tend to use an alternative expression whenever possible, usually with modal verbs (auxiliaries), to avoid the subjunctive in conversation and informal writing. Compare the following sentences with the examples above.

    *I wish that he **could come**.*
    *I told her that she **must learn** the subjunctive.*
    *It is important for him **to avoid** errors.*
    *Mary **needs to see** its importance.*

The subjunctive mood in Italian has four tenses: present, imperfect, present perfect, and past perfect.

Present subjunctive

Forms The present subjunctive is formed by dropping the -o of the first-person singular of the present tense and adding the appropriate endings from the chart below.

Verbs that end in -care or -gare add h in all forms of the present subjunctive.

The dominant vowel of the -are verbs becomes i, while the dominant vowel of both the -ere and -ire verbs becomes a.

parlare	vedere	sentire
che io parli	che io veda	che io senta
che tu parli	che tu veda	che tu senta
che lui/lei parli	che lui/lei veda	che lui/lei senta
che noi parliamo	che noi vediamo	che noi sentiamo
che voi parliate	che voi vediate	che voi sentiate
che loro parlino	che loro vedano	che loro sentano

Che is placed before the subjunctive forms above to show that these forms are used only in subordinate clauses (even if the main clause is not expressed).

It is important to use the personal pronouns for the three persons of the singular if the subject is unclear.

Several verbs whose *io* form ends in -go change the stem for the *noi* and *voi* forms in the present indicative.

cogliere	**colgo**
porre	**pongo**
rimanere	**rimango**
salire	**salgo**
scegliere	**scelgo**
spegnere	**spengo**
tenere	**tengo**
venire	**vengo**

The stems of these verbs also change in the present subjunctive.

INFINITIVE	*io* STEM	*noi/voi* STEM
porre	che io ponga	che noi poniamo, che voi poniate
venire	che io venga	che noi veniamo, che voi veniate

CONTINUED ON PAGE 118 ▶

IRREGULAR SUBJUNCTIVES Some common verbs are irregular in the present subjunctive.

INFINITIVE	IRREGULAR STEMS + ENDINGS
andare	*vada, vada, vada; andiamo, andiate, vadano*
avere	*abbia, abbia, abbia; abbiamo, abbiate, abbiano*
dare	*dia, dia, dia; diamo, diate, diano*
dire	*dica, dica, dica; diciamo, diciate, dicano*
dovere	*debba, debba, debba; dobbiamo, dobbiate, debbano*
essere	*sia, sia, sia; siamo, siate, siano*
potere	*possa, possa, possa; possiamo, possiate, possano*
sapere	*sappia, sappia, sappia; sappiamo, sappiate, sappiano*
stare	*stia, stia, stia; stiamo, stiate, stiano*
uscire	*esca, esca, esca; usciamo, usciate, escano*
volere	*voglia, voglia, voglia; vogliamo, vogliate, vogliano*

Uses In theory, the subjunctive is used to express that something is

1. potentially (but not actually) true.
2. colored by emotion (which often distorts facts).
3. an attitude about something (rather than an actual fact).
4. doubtful, probably nonexistent, or simply untrue.

In practice, there are certain words and expressions that require the subjunctive. Theory may help an Italian learner remember which ones require the subjunctive, but theory must yield to practice. If an expression requires the subjunctive, it must be used, whether or not one believes that it accords with theory.

The subjunctive is used principally

1. after verbs and expressions conveying the subject's emotional reactions.

> ***Sono contento*** *che...*
> ***Temiamo*** *che...*
> ***Mi sorprende*** *che...*

2. after verbs such as *volere, supporre, esigere,* and *credere* when there is a change of subject.

> ***Spero*** *che tu* ***venga.***

If the subject of the two clauses is the same, the infinitive is used.

> ***Spero*** *di* ***venire.***

3. after impersonal expressions when uncertainty is conveyed. Compare the sentences in the two columns of the following list.

FOLLOWED BY A SUBJUNCTIVE VERB	FOLLOWED BY AN INDICATIVE VERB
Dubito *che mio padre* ***venga.***	***Sono certo*** *che mio padre* ***viene*** *oggi.*
È possibile *che io non* ***venga.***	***È vero*** *che lei* ***ha chiamato.***
È incredibile *che loro* ***vincano.***	***È certo*** *che loro* ***hanno studiato.***
È importante *che loro* ***studino*** *l'italiano.*	***È sicuro*** *che lei mi* ***crede.***
È bene *che tu* ***vada*** *dal dottore.*	***So*** *che la bambina* ***vuole*** *la mamma.*
È necessario *che tu* ***compri*** *una macchina.*	
È improbabile *che* ***piova*** *nel deserto.*	
È meglio *che tu* ***stia*** *a letto.*	
È giusto *che* ***aspettino*** *il loro turno.*	

CONTINUED ON PAGE 119 ▶

4. after conjunctions expressing the following ideas.

CONCESSION	*dunque, benché*
PURPOSE	*purché, affinché*
INDEFINITE TIME	*finché, prima che*
NEGATION	*senza che, a meno che*

5. after superlatives (because of the possibility of exaggeration). Compare the following sentences.

> *È la poesia **più bella** che **io conosca**.*
> *È il ragazzo **più alto** che **conosco**.*

The first sentence expresses an opinion, the second expresses a fact; the subjunctive and indicative signal how a statement is meant to be understood. Some native Italian speakers do not make this distinction and use the subjunctive in every case.

6. after relative pronouns referring to an indefinite antecedent.

> *Vorrei parlare con **qualcuno che conosca** bene la città.*

7. after certain verbs (especially *pensare* and *credere*) in the negative and interrogative. (Asking what someone thinks, or saying what someone does not believe, implies doubt about the actual situation.) The negative-interrogative often takes the indicative because a positive response is expected.

> *Credi che il professore **sia** ammalato?*
> *Non credo che il professore **sia** ammalato.*
> *Non credi che il professore **sia** (or **è**) ammalato?*

8. in third-person commands (see page 115).

9. in certain fixed expressions.

***Viva** il re!*	Long live the king!
*Che Dio **ti benedica**!*	God bless you!

To remember the principal uses of the subjunctive in Italian, the mnemonic "**NEEDS PAWS**" may be used.

Necessity
Emotion
Exaggeration
Demanding
Seeming
Possibility
Asking
Wishing
Supposing

CONTINUED ON PAGE 120 ▶

HOW TO AVOID THE SUBJUNCTIVE IN ITALIAN The subjunctive is used only in subordinate clauses (even if the main clause is not expressed) and only when the subjects of the two clauses are different. If the subject is the same, the subjunctive is avoided by using

1. the infinitive. Compare the following sentences.

> *Io sono contento che voi **siate** qui.*
> *Io sono contento di **essere** qui.*

2. a modal verb. Compare the following sentences.

> *È necessario che io **vada**.*
> ***Devo** andare.*

Imperfect subjunctive

Forms The imperfect subjunctive of all regular verbs and almost all irregular verbs is formed by dropping the *-vo* of the first-person singular of the imperfect indicative and adding the tense endings.

parlare	vedere	sentire	finire
che io parlassi	che io vedessi	che io sentissi	che io finissi
che tu parlassi	che tu vedessi	che tu sentissi	che tu finissi
che lui/lei parlasse	che lui/lei vedesse	che lui/lei sentisse	che lui/lei finisse
che noi parlassimo	che noi vedessimo	che noi sentissimo	che noi finissimo
che voi parlaste	che voi vedeste	che voi sentiste	che voi finiste
che loro parlassero	che loro vedessero	che loro sentissero	che loro finissero

IRREGULAR VERBS Verbs with irregular forms in the imperfect subjunctive follow.

dare	dessi, dessi, desse; dessimo, deste, dessero
dire	dicessi, dicessi, dicesse; dicessimo, diceste, dicessero
essere	fossi, fossi, fosse; fossimo, foste, fossero
fare	facessi, facessi, facesse; facessimo, faceste, facessero
stare	stessi, stessi, stesse; stessimo, steste, stessero

Uses The imperfect subjunctive is used in subordinate clauses where

1. the verb in the main clause requires a subjunctive in the past.

*Gli studenti **temevano** che il professore* * **fosse** ammalato.*	The students were afraid that the professor was sick.

2. the verb in the main clause is in the present conditional and requires a subjunctive.

*Maria **vorrebbe** che io **venissi** a casa sua.*	Mary would like me to come to her house.

CONTINUED ON PAGE 121 ▶

Present perfect subjunctive

Forms The present perfect subjunctive is formed with the present subjunctive of the auxiliary *avere* or *essere* plus the past participle of the main verb.

parlare	*venire*
che io abbia parlato	che io sia venuto/venuta
che tu abbia parlato	che tu sia venuto/venuta
che lui/lei abbia parlato	che lui/lei sia venuto/venuta
che noi abbiamo parlato	che noi siamo venuti/venute
che voi abbiate parlato	che voi siate venuti/venute
che loro abbiano parlato	che loro siano venuti/venute

Uses The present perfect subjunctive is used in subordinate clauses that express an action that has taken place or may have taken place when that verb is governed by a verb or other expression that requires a subjunctive.

| **Spero** *che il professore* **abbia preparato** *un esame facile.* | I hope the professor has prepared an easy exam. |
| **Benché abbia piovuto** *molto, il terreno è arido.* | Even though it rained a lot, the soil is dry. |

Past perfect subjunctive

Forms The past perfect (pluperfect) subjunctive is formed with the imperfect subjunctive of the auxiliary verb *avere* or *essere* and the past participle of the main verb.

parlare	*andare*
che io avessi parlato	che io fossi andato/andata
che tu avessi parlato	che tu fossi andato/andata
che lui/lei avesse parlato	che lui/lei fosse andato/andata
che noi avessimo parlato	che noi fossimo andati/andate
che voi aveste parlato	che voi foste andati/andate
che loro avessero parlato	che loro fossero andati/andate

Uses The past perfect subjunctive is used in subordinate clauses in which the action has occurred prior to the action of the verb in the main clause.

| **Temevano** *che Maria* **fosse partita.** | They were afraid Mary had left. |
| **Non sapevo** *che* **avessero comprato** *una casa.* | I didn't know that they had bought a house. |

CONTINUED ON PAGE 122 ▶

Se-clause and the subjunctive

To express a contrary-to-fact statement in the present or future, the imperfect subjunctive is used in the *se*-clause itself. The conditional is generally used in the main clause to express a conclusion.

Se **avessi i soldi, viaggerei**.	If I had the money, I would travel.

To express a contrary-to-fact statement in the past, the perfect subjunctive is used in the *se*-clause and the conditional is used in the main clause. The conditional and present subjunctive are never used in the *se*-clause; only the imperfect and the past perfect subjunctive are used there.

Se lei mi **scrivesse**, le **risponderei**.	If she wrote me, I would answer.
Se tu mi **avessi scritto**, ti **avrei risposto**.	If you had written me, I would have answered you.

Se + the imperfect subjunctive is used in exclamations to express wishes that may never materialize.

Se **avessi** tempo!	If only I had time!
Se **sapessi** dov'è!	If only I knew where he is!

If the hypothesis is not contrary to fact, the indicative is used in the *se*-clause.

Se **vengono**, te lo dico.	If they come, I will tell you.
Se lui **arriva** presto, veniamo a teatro con voi.	If he arrives soon, we'll go to the theater with you.

Exercises

The following exercises, grouped by part of speech, test your grasp of key grammatical aspects of Italian. As a reminder of the similarities and differences between Italian and English, a cross-reference is provided at the end of each exercise to the relevant grammar points discussed in this book. An answer key is provided after the appendices.

Nouns

A *Add the correct definite article before each of the following Italian nouns.*

1. _____ classe

2. _____ libro

3. _____ acqua

4. _____ tavola

5. _____ cucchiaio

6. _____ zaino

7. _____ sport

8. _____ zii

9. _____ ombra

10. _____ ombre

◀ *For more help, see* Introducing determiners, *page 17.*

B *Complete each of the following sentences with the correct form of the definite or indefinite article.*

1. Hai sete? Ecco _____ bicchiere d'acqua.

2. C'è _____ buon ristorante qui vicino?

3. Sì, _____ ristoranti in questa città sono molto buoni.

4. Compro _____ verdure per questa sera.

5. E io, compro _____ pesce.

6. Non compri _____ fagiolini?

7. Non dimenticare di comprare _____ dolce.

8. C'è _____ ristorante italiano qui vicino?

9. _____ ristoranti italiani qui vicino, sono chiusi.

10. In quel ristorante c'è _____ brava cuoca.

◀ *For more help, see* Introducing determiners, *page 17.*

Pronouns

A *List all subject pronouns that can be used with each of the following present tense verb forms.*

1. parliamo _____

2. scrivo _____

3. vende _____

4. state _____

5. posso _____

6. crede _____

7. pongono _____

8. correte _____

9. facciamo _____

10. vivono _____

◀ *For more help, see* Personal pronouns, *page 23.*

B *Complete each of the following exchanges with the correct direct object pronoun.*

1. —Conosci quella ragazza?

   —Sì, _____ conosco bene.

2. —Inviti tutti gli amici alla festa?

   —Non so se _____ invito.

3. —Sai dove sono i ristoranti italiani in questa città?

   —No. Non _____ so.

4. —Hai sentito quella canzone?

   —Sì, _____ ho sentita, ma non mi piace.

5. —Hai chiuso la porta e le finestre prima di uscire?

   —Sì, _____ ho chiuse.

6. —Volete vedere quel film?

   —Sì, _____ vogliamo vedere. OR —Sì, vogliamo veder_____.

◀ *For more help, see* Direct object pronouns, *pages 23 and 25.*

C *Rewrite each of the following sentences, replacing the italicized phrase with the correct indirect object pronoun.*

1. Lei porta i regali *ai nipoti.*

   _____

2. Compro il vestito *a mia figlia.*

   _____

3. Vado a insegnare la matematica *alla ragazza.*

   _____

4. Spiegate *a tutti noi* dove sarà la festa.

   _____

5. Devo telefonare *a mia madre.*

   _____

6. Mando una cartolina *alla mia amica.*

   _____

7. Lavo la biancheria *di mio nipote.*

   _____

8. Compriamo la verdura *per la vecchia signora.*

   _____

9. Portiamo la frutta *a voi.*

   _____

10. Io non parlo *a quell'uomo.*

    _____

◀ *For more help, see* Indirect object pronouns, *page 25.*

D *Rewrite each of the following sentences, replacing the italicized words with the correct direct and indirect object pronouns.*

1. *Ti* porto *la torta.*

   _____

2. Compriamo *i libri per nostra nipote.*

   _____

3. Tu compri *i gioielli a tua cugina.*

   _____

4. Lei dà *la mano a noi.*

   _____

5. Il padre legge *il libro alla bambina.*

_____

6. Maria *mi* prepara *la cena* tutte le sere.

_____

7. Lui *ti* ha rotto *il bicchiere.*

_____

8. Lei dice *quello che è successo al suo amico.*

_____

9. Dico *a mio marito il risultato della partita.*

_____

10. I ragazzi *vi* raccontano *le bugie.*

_____

◀ *For more help, see* Direct object pronouns, *pages 23 and 25, and* Indirect object pronouns, *pages 25 and 27.*

E *Complete each of the following sentences with the correct form of the disjunctive pronoun.*

1. A _____ non piace questo ristorante. (me)

2. Io vado al cinema con _____. (him)

3. Io andrò in Italia con _____. (her)

4. Io penso spesso a _____. (them)

5. Ho visto soltanto _____. (you [sing.])

6. Non ho visto che _____. (you [sing.])

7. Noi pensiamo a _____. (him)

8. Fra _____ e _____ c'è di mezzo il mare. (me, you)

◀ *For more help, see* Disjunctive pronouns, *page 31.*

F *Complete each of the following Italian sentences so that they match the English sentences in meaning.*

1. I like my bicycle, but he prefers his.

   A me piace la mia bicicletta, ma lui preferisce la _____.

2. This house is older than ours.

   Questa casa è più vecchia della _____.

3. These books aren't Mary's, they're mine.

   Questi libri non sono di Maria, sono i _____.

4. She needs a pencil, because she has lost hers.

   Lei ha bisogno di una matita perché ha perso la _____.

5. Our dog is bigger than theirs.

   Il nostro cane è più grande del _____.

6. I like your class, it is better than mine.

   Mi piace la tua classe, è migliore della _____.

7. My daughter doesn't want this ring. I will give it to yours.

   Mia figlia non vuole questo anello. Lo darò alla _____.

8. I brought my tennis balls, and you brought yours.

   Io ho portato le mie palle da tennis e tu hai portato le _____.

◄ *For more help, see* Possessive pronouns, *page 27.*

G *Select the correct relative pronoun to complete each of the following sentences.*

1. Vedo l'articolo _____ hai scritto.
   a. che
   b. chi
   c. cui
   d. il quale

2. Vorrei conoscere il collega con _____ lavorerò.
   a. che
   b. il quale
   c. cui
   d. chi

3. Questi sono i bambini per i _____ ho comprato i giocattoli.
   a. quali
   b. che
   c. quale
   d. cui

4. Ti voglio mostrare il lavoro _____ ho fatto.
   a. chi
   b. che
   c. il quale
   d. cui

5. L'ingegnere _____ voi conoscete è molto intelligente.
   a. cui
   b. il quale
   c. chi
   d. che

6. Lo scrittore il _____ libro hai letto è molto famoso.
   a. che
   b. quale
   c. cui
   d. chi

7. Non capiamo _____ vuole.
   a. chi
   b. il quale
   c. a cui
   d. di cui

◀ *For more help, see* Relative pronouns, *page 33.*

Adjectives

A   *Complete the following lists with the missing forms of the adjective.*

1. a. un libro _____
   b. una storia _____
   c. libri __interessanti__
   d. storie _____

2. a. una casa __bianca__
   b. un fiore _____
   c. fiori _____
   d. case _____

3. a. un ristorante __italiano__
   b. una ricetta _____
   c. dei ristoranti _____
   d. delle ricette _____

4. a. un pacco __leggero__
   b. una valigia _____
   c. dei pacchi _____
   d. delle valigie _____

5. a. un monumento __nazionale__
   b. uno sport _____
   c. dei monumenti _____
   d. degli sport _____

6. a. una donna _____

   b. un uomo _____

   c. delle donne ___gioviali___

   d. degli uomini _____

7. a. un bambino _____

   b. una donna ___felice___

   c. dei bambini _____

   d. delle donne _____

◀ *For more help, see* Descriptive adjectives, *pages 45–47.*

B *Complete each of the following sentences with the correct form of* bello/a.

1. Voi avete un _____ appartamento.

2. È un _____ libro.

3. Mi piacciono le _____ macchine.

4. Sono dei _____ bambini.

5. Ci sono delle _____ case in questo vicinato.

6. Lei ha dei _____ occhi.

7. I miei amici hanno un _____ orto.

8. Tu hai una _____ amica.

9. Lei è una _____ ragazza.

10. Isabella ha uno _____ scoiattolino.

◀ *For more help, see* Descriptive adjectives, *page 47.*

C *Translate the following sentences into Italian.*

1. Giovanni is more intelligent than Marco.

   _____

2. My sister is less happy than my brother.

   _____

3. It is the best book in the library.

   _____

4. The subway is faster than the bus.

   _____

5. My course is less interesting than theirs.

   _____

6. This car is as beautiful as yours (pl.).

_____

7. Your car is not as fast as mine.

_____

8. She is more beautiful than intelligent.

_____

9. You (formal pl.) are very educated.

_____

10. You (fem.) are the best student of the class.

_____

◀ *For more help, see* Comparison of adjectives, *page 49.*

D *Translate the following phrases into Italian.*

1. her book _____

2. my house _____

3. their garden _____

4. my program _____

5. his life _____

6. her work _____

7. your (sing.) homework _____

8. his suit _____

9. her suit _____

◀ *For more help, see* Possessive adjectives, *page 53.*

Adverbs

A *Write the adverb that corresponds to each of the following adjectives.*

1. facile _____

2. rapido _____

3. lento _____

4. certo _____

5. felice _____

6. vago _____

7. chiaro _____

8. meraviglioso _____

9. serio _____

10. feroce _____

◀ *For more help, see* Introducing adverbs, *page 61.*

Prepositions

A   *Add the correct preposition before each of the following geographical names.*

1. Hanno una casa _____ California.

2. Questa estate andremo _____ Italia.

3. Ho trovato un lavoro _____ Roma.

4. I suoi amici sono _____ Canada.

5. Sono _____ Montreal.

6. Ho uno zio _____ Stati Uniti.

7. Lavora _____ Chicago.

8. Non so quando ritornerà _____ Europa.

9. Questa estate vado _____ Sicilia.

10. I miei amici si sposano _____ isole Hawaii.

◀ *For more help, see* Introducing prepositions, *page 77.*

B   *Add the correct contracted preposition in each of the following sentences.*

1. La casa _____ nonna è bella, ma vecchia.

2. Lavoro vicino _____ metropolitana.

3. Ha dimenticato i libri _____ macchina.

4. Oggi ho male _____ stomaco.

5. Questa è la casa _____ zii.

6. La vita _____ senzatetto è molto dura.

7. Ritorna _____ lavoro molto tardi.

8. Deve lavorare _____ otto di mattina fino _____ sette di sera.

9. Il nido _____ scoiattolo è _____ alberi.

10. Ci sono molti bambini _____ mio quartiere.

◀ *For more help, see* Introducing prepositions, *page 75.*

Verbs

A *Complete the following chart with the present and past participles of each infinitive.*

INFINITIVE	PRESENT PARTICIPLE	PAST PARTICIPLE
1. camminare	_____	_____
2. scegliere	_____	_____
3. avere	_____	_____
4. leggere	_____	_____
5. arrivare	_____	_____
6. essere	_____	_____
7. pulire	_____	_____
8. comprare	_____	_____
9. scendere	_____	_____
10. sapere	_____	_____
11. bere	_____	_____
12. dire	_____	_____
13. nascere	_____	_____
14. vedere	_____	_____
15. fare	_____	_____

◀ *For more help, see* Participles, *pages 87 and 89.*

B *Complete each of the following sentences with the correct present tense form of the verb in parentheses.*

1. (camminare) Lui _____ velocemente.

2. (scegliere) Noi _____ dei regali per il suo compleanno.

3. (finire) Lei non _____ mai il suo lavoro.

4. (cantare) Tu _____ bene.

5. (vendere) Chi _____ questi libri?

6. (guardare) Voi _____ molti film.

7. (fare) Loro non _____ mai niente.

8. (imparare) I bambini _____ molto velocemente.

9. (arrivare) Se voi _____ presto, possiamo andare al parco.

10. (partire)   Il treno _____ in orario.

11. (chiudere)   Lui _____ sempre le finestre.

12. (salire)   La bambina _____ sempre sul tavolo.

13. (scendere)   Loro _____ le scale di corsa.

14. (spingere)   La mamma _____ la carrozzina.

15. (piovere)   Nella giungla _____ sempre.

◀ *For more help, see* Present tense, *pages 91 and 93.*

C *Rewrite the following sentences, using the imperfect tense.*

1. Lui parla con la sua fidanzata.

   _____

2. Lei prende un caffè tutte le mattine.

   _____

3. Il bambino dorme.

   _____

4. Noi siamo stanchi.

   _____

5. Tu vendi la casa.

   _____

6. Loro lavorano in un ufficio grande.

   _____

7. Studiamo la lezione di piano.

   _____

8. Lui deve partire presto.

   _____

9. Voi mangiate all'una.

   _____

10. Tu scrivi una lettera.

    _____

◀ *For more help, see* Imperfect tense, *pages 95–96.*

D *Complete each of the following sentences with the correct future tense form of the verb(s) in parentheses.*

1. (andare)   Lui _____ in Italia.

2. (avere)   Io _____ molto da fare.

3. (partire)   A che ora _____ tu?

4. (mandare)   Io ti _____ un regalo.

5. (essere)   Loro _____ molto felici di vederti.

6. (aspettare)   Voi mi _____ vero?

7. (acquistare, essere)   Lei _____ le scarpe quando

                             _____ in Italia.

8. (cadere)   Noi non _____ sul ghiaccio.

9. (uscire)   A che ora _____ voi?

10. (raccogliere)   Questa estate noi _____ le ciliegie.

◀ *For more help, see* Future tense, *page 99.*

E *Complete each of the following sentences with the correct conditional form of the verb in parentheses.*

1. (andare)   Se io avessi l'occasione, _____ ad imparare a sciare.

2. (parlare)   Loro _____ l'italiano se l'avessero studiato.

3. (fare)   Lei _____ la torta se tu glielo chiedessi.

4. (fare)   Se avessimo tempo, ti _____ una visita.

5. (volere)   Dicono che _____ andare al cinema con noi, se andiamo di sera.

6. (aprire)   Se fosse caldo, io _____ le finestre.

7. (togliere)   Se avessi caldo, mi _____ la giacca.

8. (ballare)   Io _____ se ci fosse la musica.

9. (rispondere) Lei pensa che lui _____ se tu lo chiamassi.

10. (scegliere)   Io _____ un buon avvocato se avessi i soldi.

◀ *For more help, see* Conditional tense, *page 101.*

F *Complete each of the following sentences with the correct present perfect form of the verb in parentheses.*

1. (servire)   Io _____ un pasto delizioso.

2. (entrare)   Lei _____ in classe.

3. (prendere)   Noi _____ un caffè al bar vicino a casa.

4. (nascere)   Il primo nipotino di Carolina _____ in luglio.

5. (fare)   Noi _____ colazione in campagna.

6. (ritornare)   Tu _____ a casa troppo tardi.

7. (camminare)   Voi _____ per un'ora.

8. (lavarsi)   I signori si _____ le mani prima di mangiare.

9. (finire)   I ragazzi _____ la partita.

10. (arrivare)   I nonni _____ la settimana scorsa.

◀ *For more help, see* Present perfect tense, *pages 103 and 105.*

G   *Complete each of the following sentences with the correct present subjunctive form of the verb in parentheses.*

1. (dormire)   Penso che tu _____ troppo poco.

2. (aspettare)   Non credo che lei ti _____.

3. (prendere)   Voglio che voi _____ un caffè.

4. (venire)   È possibile che lei _____ con il suo amico.

5. (piovere)   È probabile che domani _____.

6. (ritornare)   Penso che lui _____ a casa.

7. (sapere)   Non è possibile che lui _____ la verità.

8. (passare)   Desideriamo che voi _____ da casa nostra dopo il lavoro.

9. (piovere)   Spero che domani non _____.

10. (stare)   Desideriamo che voi _____ da noi quando venite in America.

◀ *For more help, see* Present subjunctive, *pages 117–119.*

H   *Complete each of the following sentences with the correct imperfect subjunctive form of the verb in parentheses.*

1. (venire)   Non era molto probabile che loro _____ da noi.

2. (sapere)   Credevamo che voi lo _____.

3. (studiare)   Era necessario che lui _____ di più.

4. (cantare)   Vorrei che lui _____ per noi.

5. (essere)   Speravo che la casa _____ più moderna.

6. (decidere)   Hanno insistito perché lei _____ di operarsi.

7. (volere)   Non sapeva che cosa io _____.

8. (ritornare)   Vorremmo che voi _____.

9. (saltare)   Non volevo che loro _____ sul divano.

10. (ritornare)   Lei sperava che noi _____ a casa presto.

◀ *For more help, see* Imperfect subjunctive, *page 120.*

I *Complete each of the following sentences with the correct present perfect or past perfect subjunctive form of the verb in parentheses.*

1. (andare)   Non sapevo che loro _____ in vacanza con voi.

2. (sapere)   Se lo _____, saremmo venuti.

3. (rispondere)   Speravo che lui _____ già alla tua lettera.

4. (arrivare)   Spero che loro _____ in orario.

5. (mandare)   Mi sarebbe piaciuto che lui _____ le fotografie della bambina.

6. (arrivare)   Speravamo che loro _____.

7. (mettere)   Credevo che loro _____ le cinture di sicurezza.

8. (riparare)   Pensavamo che lui _____ la finestra.

9. (comprare)   Spero che tu _____ una bicicletta nuova.

10. (prendere)   Lui credeva che tu _____ la patente l'anno scorso.

◀ *For more help, see* Present perfect subjunctive, *page 121, and* Past perfect subjunctive, *page 121.*

J *Complete each of the following sentences with the correct subjunctive form of the verb in parentheses.*

1. (volere)   Io credo che voi _____ andare a dormire presto.

2. (essere)   Lui pensava che lei _____ già in macchina.

3. (venire)   Loro vorrebbero che io _____ in ufficio presto.

4. (portare)   È possibile che lei mi _____ il libro di cui ho bisogno?

5. (arrivare)   Era impossibile che tu _____ così presto.

6. (avere mangiato)   Penso che voi _____ in treno.

7. (avere mangiato)   Credevo che voi _____ in treno.

8. (avere comprato)   Noi pensavamo che voi _____ un altro cane.

9. (avere)   Verremmo in Italia se _____ una casa.

10. (conoscere)   Sarei puntuale se _____ la strada.

11. (essere)   Mangeresti la frutta se _____ matura.

12. (avere cotto)   Avresti mangiato la pasta se io l'_____.

◀ *For more help, see* Subjunctive mood, *pages 117–122.*

Interrogative pronouns and adjectives—a comparison

Interrogative pronouns *chi?, che?, quale?, quanto?*

Chi? means "who?" *Che?* means "what?" *Quale?/quali?* means "which?" or "which ones?" *Quanto?/quanta?/quanti?/quante?* means "how much?" or "how many?"

Che / Che cosa leggi?	What are you reading?
Quale/Quali di questi libri vuoi leggere?	Which of these books do you want to read?

With the verb *essere*, *chi?*, *che?*, and *quale?/quali?* ask for information.

Chi è questa ragazza?	Who is this girl?
Chi di voi è italiano?	Who among you is Italian?
Che è un mango?	What is a mango?
Quale è il tuo libro?	Which one is your book?
Quale è la ragazza nuova?	Which one is the new girl?

Cui is an invariable relative pronoun. It is often preceded by a preposition or a definite article.

La signora a cui parlo è americana.	The woman to whom I am speaking is American.
La città da cui vengo è grande.	The city I come from is large.
Le persone con cui viaggio sono interessanti.	The people I am traveling with are interesting.
La signora di cui ti ho parlato è molto gentile.	The woman I told you about is very kind.
Il signore per cui lavoro è molto intelligente.	The man I work for is very intelligent.
Conosco la signora il cui figlio lavora qui.	I know the woman whose son works here.

Interrogative adjectives *che?, quale?, quanto?*

When *che?*, *quale?/quali?*, and *quanto?/quanta?/quanti?/quante?* accompany a noun, they function as adjectives, even though they have the same form as the interrogative pronouns.

Che libro leggi?	What book are you reading?
Quale libro preferisci?	Which book do you prefer?
Quanti giornali compri?	How many newspapers do you buy?

Che? implies an unlimited choice, while *quale?* implies a limited one.

Che *libri ti piacciono?*	What books do you like?
Quale *libro preferisci? Questo o quello?*	Which book do you prefer? This one or that one?

With the verb *essere, quale?/quali?* asks for information about the noun.

Quali *sono i titoli dei tuoi libri preferiti?*	What are the titles of your favorite books?

APPENDIX B

The pronouns *ci* and *ne*

Ci

The pronoun *ci* refers to objects or places and usually replaces a prepositional phrase.

*Quando andate **in Italia**? **Ci** andiamo questa estate.*

When will you go to Italy? We'll go there this summer.

*Con chi vai **dal dottore**? **Ci** vado con mio marito.*

With whom will you go to the doctor? I will go with my husband.

Ci can mean "to it/them," "in it/them," or "on it/them" when the place is already known.

*Andate **al cinema**? Sì, **ci** andiamo oggi.*

Will you go to the movies? Yes, we'll go today.

Ci is used in many idiomatic expressions, such as *crederci, esserci, metterci, pensarci,* and *entrarci.*

*Prima di decidere dove andare, devi **pensarci** bene.*

Before deciding where to go, you must think about it.

Ne

The pronoun *ne* refers to people, places, or things previously mentioned in a sentence. It replaces *di* + noun and means "some," "any," "of it/them," etc.

*Maria compra **delle paste**. Maria **ne** compra alcune.*

Mary buys some pastries. Mary buys a few of them.

Ne replaces nouns accompanied by a number, as well as expressions of capacity, such as *molto, troppo,* and *un chilogrammo.*

*Quanti **figli** hai? **Ne** ho due.*

How many kids do you have? I have two.

Ne replaces *di* + infinitive in expressions with *avere bisogno di, avere paura di,* and *avere voglia di.*

*Hanno bisogno **di prendere dei soldi**? Sì, **ne** hanno bisogno.*

Do they need to get some money? Yes, they do.

Ne is placed before the conjugated verb, as are direct and indirect object pronouns.

*Luisa **ne** vuole due.*

Luisa wants two of them.

Ne may also be attached to an infinitive.

*Carla vuole mangiar**ne**.*

Carla wants to eat some of them.

In compound tenses, *ne* usually agrees with the past participle only when it replaces a partitive noun. When *ne* is used with numbers, there is no agreement.

*Ho comprato **delle banane**. **Ne** ho **comprate** un kilo.*	I bought a few bananas. I bought a kilo.
*Hai letto **dei libri interessanti**? Sì, **ne** ho **letto** due o tre.*	Did you read any interesting books? Yes, I have read two or three.

APPENDIX C
Commands

Familiar commands

parla!	*scrivi!*	*senti!*	*finisci!*
parliamo!	*scriviamo!*	*sentiamo!*	*finiamo!*
parlate!	*scrivete!*	*sentite!*	*finite!*

Negative familiar commands

non parlare!	*non scrivere!*	*non sentire!*	*non finire!*
non parliamo!	*non scriviamo!*	*non sentiamo!*	*non finiamo!*
non parlate!	*non scrivete!*	*non sentite!*	*non finite!*

Formal commands

Lei parli!	*Lei scriva!*	*Lei senta!*	*Lei finisca!*
Loro parlino!	*Loro scrivano!*	*Loro sentano!*	*Loro finiscano!*

Negative formal commands are formed by placing *non* before the verb.

Irregular commands

INFINITIVE	INFORMAL COMMAND	SINGULAR FORMAL COMMAND	PLURAL FORMAL COMMAND
andare	*va'* OR *vai*	*vada*	*vadano*
avere	*abbi*	*abbia*	*abbiano*
bere	*bevi*	*beva*	*bevano*
dare	*da'* OR *dai*	*dia*	*diano*
dire	*di'*	*dica*	*dicano*
essere	*sii*	*sia*	*siano*
fare	*fa'* OR *fai*	*faccia*	*facciano*
stare	*sta'* OR *stai*	*stia*	*stiano*
temere	*temi*	*tema*	*temano*
venire	*vieni*	*venga*	*vengano*

Determiners

DETERMINERS FOR WORDS BEGINNING WITH A CONSONANT

MASCULINE		FEMININE	
SINGULAR	PLURAL	SINGULAR	PLURAL
il caffè, un caffè	*i caffè, i libri*	*la chiesa,* *una chiesa*	*le chiese, le case*
lo zio, lo stagno	*gli zii, gli stagni*		
il mio caffè, *il tuo libro*	*i miei caffè,* *i tuoi libri*	*la mia chiesa,* *la tua casa*	*le mie chiese,* *le tue case*
	tre caffè, tre tavoli		*tre chiese, tre case*
questo caffè	*questi libri*	*questa casa*	*queste signore*
quel fiore	*quei fiori*	*quella gatta*	*quelle piante*
quello zaino, *quello studente*	*quegli zaini,* *quegli studenti*		
qualche caffè		*qualche casa*	
del caffè, del pane	*dei panini, dei fiori*	*della frutta*	*delle patate*

DETERMINERS FOR WORDS BEGINNING WITH A VOWEL OR *h*

MASCULINE		FEMININE	
SINGULAR	PLURAL	SINGULAR	PLURAL
l'orto, l'hotel *un orto, un hotel*	*gli orti, gli hotel*	*l'amica, l'acqua* *un'amica, un'oca*	*le amiche, le acque*
quest'orto, *quest'amico*	*questi orti,* *questi amici*	*quest'amica,* *quest'acqua*	*queste amiche,* *queste acque*

No determiner is required

1. after some prepositions, for example, *senza* (*senza dubbio*).

2. when a noun of nationality, profession, or religion is used as an adjective, for example, *è americano*.

3. when one noun is used to describe another, for example, *un professore d'arte, una festa di famiglia*.

4. when a proper name is used in possession, for example, *l'amico di Enrico*.

5. in a partitive construction under certain circumstances (see page 17).

Expressions with *avere* and *fare*

Avere

The verb *avere* is used in many idiomatic expressions in Italian. Before nouns and adjectives, the infinitive *avere* may be shortened to *aver*.

avere/aver _____ *anni*	to be _____ years old
aver caldo/freddo/fame/sete	to be warm/cold/hungry/thirsty
avere sonno	to be sleepy
aver mal (di) testa/denti	to have a headache/toothache
aver fretta	to be in a hurry
aver paura (di)	to be afraid (of)
aver voglia (di)	to feel like
aver bisogno di	to need

Abbiamo caldo, **abbiamo bisogno dell'***aria condizionata.*	We are warm, we need the air conditioning.
Hanno voglia di *andare a vedere un bel film.*	They feel like going to see a good movie.
Lei **ha fame**, *ma non può mangiare perché* **ha mal di** *denti.*	She is hungry, but she cannot eat, because she has a toothache.

Fare

The verb *fare* is used in many idiomatic expressions in Italian. The infinitive of *fare* is often shortened to *far* before a consonant.

fare attenzione	to pay attention
fare il bagno	to take a bath
fare bel/brutto tempo	to be good/bad weather
fare benzina	to get gas
fare colazione	to have breakfast
fare una domanda	to ask a question
fare una fotografia	to take a picture
fare presto	to hurry up
fare un regalo	to give a gift
fare la spesa	to get groceries
fare un viaggio	to take a trip

Lui non capisce perché non **fa attenzione**.	He does not understand, because he does not pay attention.
Lei **fa il bagno** *tutte le sere.*	She takes a bath every night.
Quando viaggio, **faccio** *tante* **fotografie**.	When I travel, I take a lot of pictures.
Mi piace **fare un regalo** *alle mie amiche.*	I like giving presents to my friends.

Answer key

Nouns

A   1. la   2. il   3. l' (la)   4. la   5. il   6. lo   7. lo   8. gli   9. l' (la)   10. le

B   1. un   2. un   3. i   4. le   5. il   6. i   7. il   8. un   9. I   10. una

Pronouns

A   1. noi   2. io   3. lui, lei   4. voi   5. io   6. lui, lei   7. loro   8. voi   9. noi   10. loro

B   1. la   2. li   3. lo   4. l' (la)   5. le   6. lo, lo

C   1. Lei gli porta i regali.   2. Le compro il vestito.   3. Vado a insegnarle la matematica.
4. Spiegateci dove sarà la festa.   5. Le devo telefonare.   6. Le mando una cartolina.
7. Gli lavo la biancheria.   8. Le compriamo la verdura.   9. Vi portiamo la frutta.
10. Io non gli parlo.

D   1. Te la porto.   2. Glieli compriamo.   3. Tu glieli compri.   4. Lei ce la dà.
5. Il padre glielo legge.   6. Maria me la prepara tutte le sere.   7. Lui te l'ha rotto.
8. Lei glielo dice.   9. Glielo dico.   10. I ragazzi ve le raccontano.

E   1. me   2. lui   3. lei   4. loro   5. te   6. te   7. lui   8. me, te

F   1. sua   2. nostra   3. miei   4. sua   5. loro   6. mia   7. tua   8. tue

G   1. a   2. c   3. a   4. b   5. d   6. c   7. a

Adjectives

A   1a. interessante   1b. interessante   1d. interessanti   2b. bianco   2c. bianchi
2d. bianche   3b. italiana   3c. italiani   3d. italiane   4b. leggera   4c. leggeri
4d. leggere   5b. nazionale   5c. nazionali   5d. nazionali   6a. gioviale   6b. gioviale
6d. gioviali   7a. felice   7c. felici   7d. felici

B   1. bell' (bello)   2. bel   3. belle   4. bei   5. belle   6. begli   7. bell' (bello)
8. bell' (bella)   9. bella   10. bello

C   1. Giovanni è più intelligente di Marco.   2. Mia sorella è meno felice di mio fratello.
3. È il miglior libro nella biblioteca.   4. La metropolitana è più veloce dell'autobus.
5. Il mio corso è meno interessante del loro.   6. Questa macchina è tanto bella quanto
la vostra.   7. La tua macchina non è tanto veloce quanto la mia.   8. Lei è più bella che
intelligente.   9. Loro sono molto istruiti.   10. Tu sei la migliore studente della classe.

D   1. il suo libro   2. la mia casa   3. il loro giardino   4. il mio programma   5. la sua vita
       6. il suo lavoro   7. il tuo compito   8. il suo vestito   9. il suo vestito

Adverbs

A   1. facilmente   2. rapidamente   3. lentamente   4. certamente   5. felicemente
       6. vagamente   7. chiaramente   8. meravigliosamente   9. seriamente   10. ferocemente

Prepositions

A   1. in   2. in   3. a   4. in   5. a   6. negli   7. a   8. in   9. in   10. alle

B   1. della   2. alla   3. nella   4. allo   5. degli   6. dei   7. dal   8. dalle, alle   9. dello, sugli
       10. nel

Verbs

A   1. camminando, camminato   2. scegliendo, scelto   3. avendo, avuto   4. leggendo, letto
       5. arrivando, arrivato   6. essendo, stato   7. pulendo, pulito   8. comprando, comprato
       9. scendendo, sceso   10. sapendo, saputo   11. bevendo, bevuto   12. dicendo, detto
       13. nascendo, nato   14. vedendo, visto   15. facendo, fatto

B   1. cammina   2. scegliamo   3. finisce   4. canti   5. vende   6. guardate   7. fanno
       8. imparano   9. arrivate   10. parte   11. chiude   12. sale   13. scendono   14. spinge
       15. piove

C   1. Lui parlava con la sua fidanzata.   2. Lei prendeva un caffè tutte le mattine.
       3. Il bambino dormiva.   4. Noi eravamo stanchi.   5. Tu vendevi la casa.
       6. Loro lavoravano in un ufficio grande.   7. Studiavamo la lezione di piano.
       8. Lui doveva partire presto.   9. Voi mangiavate all'una.   10. Tu scrivevi una lettera.

D   1. andrà   2. avrò   3. partirai   4. manderò   5. saranno   6. aspetterete
       7. acquisterà, sarà   8. cadremo   9. uscirete   10. raccoglieremo

E   1. andrei   2. parlerebbero   3. farebbe   4. farei   5. vorrebbero   6. aprirei
       7. toglierei   8. ballerei   9. risponderebbe   10. sceglierei

F   1. ho servito   2. è entrata   3. abbiamo preso   4. è nato   5. abbiamo fatto
       6. sei ritornato   7. avete camminato   8. sono lavati   9. hanno finito   10. sono arrivati

G   1. dorma   2. aspetti   3. prendiate   4. venga   5. piova   6. ritorni   7. sappia
       8. passiate   9. piova   10. stiate

H   1. venissero   2. sapeste   3. studiasse   4. cantasse   5. fosse   6. decidesse   7. volessi
       8. ritornaste   9. saltassero   10. ritornassimo

I   1. fossero andati   2. avessimo saputo   3. avesse risposto   4. siano arrivati
       5. avesse mandato   6. fossero arrivati   7. avessero messo   8. avesse riparato
       9. abbia comprato   10. avessi preso

J   1. vogliate   2. fosse   3. venissi   4. porti   5. arrivassi   6. abbiate mangiato
       7. aveste mangiato   8. aveste comprato   9. avessimo   10. conoscessi   11. fosse
       12. avessi cotta